KU-532-892

Monet

Matthias Arnold

translated by Anne Wyburd

HAUS PUBLISHING • LONDON

Dedicated to the painter Luise Niedermaier (1908-1997)
in recollection and admiration

First published in Great Britain in 2005 by
Haus Publishing Limited
26 Cadogan Court
London SW3 3BX

Originally published under the title CLAUDE MONET in the series
"rowohlts monographien"
Copyright © 1998 by Rowohlt Taschenbuch Verlag GmbH, Reinbek bei
Hamburg

English translation © Anne Wyburd, 2005

The moral right of the author has been asserted

A CIP catalogue record for this book
is available from the British Library

ISBN 1-904950-00-0 (paperback)

Designed and typeset in Garamond by Andrea El-Akshar, Köln
Printed and bound by Graphicom in Vicenza, Italy

Front cover: Courtesy of akg-Images
Back cover: Courtesy of akg-Images

CONDITIONS OF SALE
All rights reserved. No part of this publication may be reproduced, stored
in a retrieval system, or transmitted in any form or by any means, electronic,
mechanical, photocopying, recording or otherwise, without the prior
permission of the publisher

This book is sold subject to the condition that it shall not, by way of trade
or otherwise, be lent, re-sold, hired out or otherwise circulated without the
publisher's prior consent in any form of binding or cover other than that in
which it is published and without a similar condition including this condition
being imposed on the subsequent purchaser

Contents

KIRKLEES METROPOLITAN COUNCIL	
250578767	
Bertrams	29.11.05
759.4MON MON	£9.99
	CUL40491

The Pavé at Chailly, Forest of Fontainebleau, 1865. Musée d'Orsay, Paris

Claude Monet

The most wonderful Eye

Today he holds an unchallenged place among classical painters. Claude Monet was not only the most important Impressionist, he was absolutely one of the greatest exponents in his field. The praise from his highly critical friend Paul Cézanne is universally valid: 'Monet is an eye, the most wonderful eye since painters existed.'[1]

After the restoration of the garden at Giverny, through which the tourists now stream, the serial pictures he painted there in the second half of his creative life were rediscovered and grew enormously in repute, furthered not least by the publication of countless books.[2] To a great extent this comprehensive, almost emphatic, reappraisal is the result of superficial connoisseurship. Fashionable judgement threatens to gloss over Monet's main achievement, which actually consists of the exemplary impressionistic single paintings of his first creative period. Even the later serial pictures of the master of Giverny build on the revolutionary achievements of his early and middle years. Certainly the later, mature Monet was spared the fate of many colleagues who were artistically neglected in their old age: after creating a thousand single impressionistic paintings, he embarked on another, second œuvre, consisting of yet another thousand serial pictures.

Unlike Camille Pissarro, Alfred Sisley, Paul Cézanne and Vincent van Gogh, Monet was finally able to enjoy recognition and material success. Perhaps his rugged physique and impressive imperturbability helped him to survive the great privations of previous decades. However, Monet the man long remained largely hidden behind the pictures in spite of the quantity of evidence he left about himself,[3] which – together with other contemporary sources – bear witness to a strong but contradictory character. Monet combined in himself both admirable and less agreeable qualities: he was depressive and euphoric, miserly and spendthrift, opportunist and uncompromising, wilful and yielding, inconsiderate and ready to help. Having as a young painter ambitiously planned his career, fame – when it eventually came – meant hardly anything to him.

The history of Impressionism has been excellently documented[4] and will not be rehearsed yet again in these pages. The intention is rather to make Monet, man and painter, more accessible through critical presentation and interpretation.

The Man: Obstinacy and Contradictions

CHILDHOOD AND YOUTH

Even the painter's birthplace is a symbol or omen: Oscar-Claude Monet came into the world on 14 November 1849 at No 45 Rue Laffite, Paris – the street in which the most important French art dealers were later to be found. It is also remarkable that Monet's birth came just two days after that of Auguste Rodin, the greatest impressionist sculptor, with whom the greatest impressionist painter was later on friendly terms and with whom he shared exhibitions.

Oscar-Claude's older brother Léon-Pascal was born in 1836. Their parents, Claude-Adolphe Monet (1800-1871) and Louise-Justine Aubré (1805-1857) were both native Parisians. The father ran a business, though virtually nothing is known about it. The artistic blood in Oscar (for so he was called at home) must have come from his musical mother.

Clearly his father's business was going badly, because when Oscar was five years old the Monet family moved from Paris to Le Havre, where Adolphe's half-sister Marie-Jeanne Gaillard lived with her husband, Jacques Lecadre, who was a wholesale grocer. Adolphe Monet was content at first to be a salaried employee in Lecadre's flourishing business, and later apparently became manager. With his wife and sons he moved into a substantial house, 30 Rue d'Epréméril, and there Oscar grew up.

On 1 April 1851, at the age of ten, Oscar entered the public high school in Le Havre, in which the community art school was also housed. The boy was not a particularly good pupil, because most of the teaching material was of little interest to him. Sometimes he even played truant. His class teacher was a Monsieur Blanchard but it was the art-master, François-Charles Ochard – a former pupil of Jacques-Louis David who also ran the art school – who was more important to him.

In an interview he gave in 1900, the 60-year old Claude Monet, by now a recognised and well-off painter, looked back on his youth: *I am a Parisian from Paris. I was born there in 1840, under good King Louis-Philippe, in a milieu entirely given over to commerce, where everyone professed a contemptuous disdain for the arts. But I grew up in Le Havre, where my father had settled in 1845 to pursue his career, and my youth was essentially that of a vagabond. I was undisciplined by birth; never would I bend, even in my most tender youth, to a rule. It was at home that I learned the little I know. School always seemed to me like a prison, and I made up my mind to never stay there (even for four hours a day) when the sunshine was inviting, the sea was smooth, and it was such a joy to run about on the cliffs in the fresh air or to paddle around in the water.*

Until I was 14 or 15 years old, I led this unbridled but thoroughly wholesome life, to the disappointment of my poor father. Between times I had picked up in a haphazard way the rudiments of arithmetic and a smattering of orthography. This was the limit of my studies. They were not over tiresome for they were intermingled for me with distractions. I made wreaths in the margins of my textbooks; I decorated the blue paper of my copybooks with ultra-fantastical ornamentation, reproducing the faces and profiles of my masters in the most irreverent fashion, as distorted as I could.

I soon became very skilled at this pastime. At 15 I was known all over Le Havre as a caricaturist. My reputation was so well established that I was sought after from all sides and asked for portraits. The abundance of orders and the insufficiency of the subsidies derived from maternal generosity inspired me with a bold resolve which naturally scandalised my family: I took money for my portraits. According to the appearance of my clients, I charged 10 or 20 francs for each portrait and the scheme worked beautifully. In a month my patrons had doubled in number. I was now able to charge 20 francs in all cases without the number of orders decreasing. If I had kept on, I would today be a millionaire.[5]

Apart from the fact that even without a career as a caricaturist he was already a very wealthy man at the time he said this, some of his remarks may well have been examples of self-dramatisation, to make himself retrospectively sound heroic. We shall meet this phenomenon again, several times. For example, it is unimaginable that a pupil who perpetually played truant would not have been promptly expelled from school. In fact, he probably only *occasionally* missed his lessons. One cannot entirely accept that he was ill-educated, either; his letters bear witness to his having learned more than *a smattering of orthography*, and he was later a regular reader of newspapers and books. Also, that his father was *disappointed* about his *unbridled* life does not agree with the facts as we know them and with the picture we have of a very hard-hearted, even tyrannical head of the family. The 60-year-old Monet undoubtedly described his youth in this subjective way in order to portray himself as independent and strong-willed from his earliest days.

Certainly he very soon knew what he wanted – or in any case what he did *not* want: a business career such as his father had in mind was always out of the question for him, although he had a certain head for business, as demonstrated by his skill in pricing his early caricatures and by many instances in his commercial dealings later in life.

His drawing and selling of caricatures brought him not only money which he put aside, but also his first 'fame'. When he was 60 he also recalled: *Having gained consideration by these means, I was soon an important personage in the town. In the show-window of the only frame-maker who was able to make his living in Le Havre, five or six of my caricatures were prominently displayed in a row, framed in gold and* glazed, like highly artistic works, and when I saw passers-by crowd in front of them in admiration and heard them point out the subjects, saying 'That is so and so', I nearly choked with vanity and self-satisfaction.

Still there was a shadow to all this brilliance. Often in the same show-window I saw, hung above my own creations, marine paintings that I, like most of my fellow-citizens, thought disgusting. And, at heart, I was much vexed to have to endure this proximity, and never ceased to abuse the idiot who, thinking he was an artist, had enough self-complacency to sign them. This idiot was Boudin. In my eyes, accustomed as they were to the marine paintings of Gudin, to arbitrary colouration, the false notes and fantastical arrangements of the painters in vogue, the sincere little compositions of Boudin, with his realistic little figures, his ships accurately rigged, his exact skies and water, drawn and painted only from nature, were not at all artistic, and their fidelity struck me as more than suspicious. His paint-ing therefore inspired me with an intense aversion, and without knowing the man I hated him. Often the frame-maker would say to me: 'You should make the acquaintance of Mr Boudin. You see, whatever they may say of him, he knows his trade. He studied in Paris, in the studios of the École des Beaux-Arts. He could give you some good advice.' And I resisted with silly pride. What indeed could such a ridiculous man teach me?

Still the day came, the fateful day, when chance brought me, in spite of myself, face to face with Boudin. He was in the rear of the shop, and not noticing him there, I came in. The frame-maker grasped the opportunity and without consulting me presented me to him. 'Just see, Mr Boudin, this is the young man who has so much talent for caricature'. Boudin, without hesitation, came up to me, complimented me in his gentle voice and said: 'I always look at your sketches with much pleasure,; they are amusing, clever, bright. You are gifted; one can see that at a glance. But I hope you are not going to stop at that. It is all very well for a beginning, but soon you will have enough of caricaturing. Study, learn to see and to paint, draw, make landscapes. They are so beautiful, the sea and the sky, the animals, the people and the trees, just as nature has made them, with their character, their true existence in the light and the air, just as they really are'.

But the exhortations of Boudin did not take root. I did in fact like the man. I felt he was earnest and sincere but I could not tolerate his painting, and when he offered to take me with him to sketch in the fields, I always found a pretext to decline politely. Summer came and my time was my own, so I could make no valid excuse and, weary of resisting, I gave in at last. Boudin, with untiring kindness, undertook my education. My eyes, finally, were opened, and I really understood nature; I learned at the same time to love it. I analysed it in its forms with a pencil, I studied it in its colours.[6]

Here too Monet was probably exaggerating in his old age. As middle-class young man he would not have behaved so ungraciously towards an adult painter who met him with kindness and appreciation. In Le Havre, at the mouth of the Seine, Eugéne Boudin (1824-1898) painted bathers, the sea, beaches filled with people and ports with ships. All his life he remained faithful to this narrow range of subjects, which is why he is dismissed today as a one-sided and therefore second-class 'minor painter'. His delicate, fragrant water-colours and his small oil-paintings do not shout at one but present a quiet world dominated by water and sky, though admittedly painted in a spontaneous style which was ahead of his time and caught the atmosphere enchantingly.

Understandably, young Oscar Monet, who had been learning conventional art in this provincial town, at first could not acclimatise himself to this kind of painting. His reservations concerning Boudin sprang from his youthful ignorance of the revolutionary trends which had started some years before. His art-master at school and at the community art school, where he attended additional classes, was probably teaching academic classicism, from which Oscar, presumably rejecting it instinctively, turned to a 'career' as a caricaturist.

Around the time when he first encountered Boudin personally – 1856/57 – he had left the high school without a diploma. At the age of 16 he now had more time to apply himself to painting. In contrast to his later assertions, he probably unreservedly welcomed Boudin's offer to teach him. From his recollections it is not sufficiently clear when and how he changed his harsh opinion of the older man's painting. Probably this happened during their joint painting sessions, which now began in the open air on the Normandy coast near the mouth of the Seine. The young Monet probably accompanied Boudin to his chosen subjects where he also made his first attempts at painting, of which virtually nothing has survived. Boudin advised and instructed him, and taught him for the first time how to look at a landscape properly. The passionate landscape-painter and important Impressionist-to-be could have found no better teacher; chance had thrown together two artists who were made for one another. There is no doubt that Monet gained more from the connection than Boudin yet, especially in his later years, the older man was also fruitfully stimulated by his exceptional 'pupil'.

In his 70s Monet completed the description of his first collaboration with Boudin: *But I ran into Boudin again at the framer's. 'So', he said, 'you don't want to come along with me.' What did I have to lose? It would be amusing; I told myself it would be fun. So, one day I joined Boudin in painting out-of-doors. I began to daub my canvas. Then I watched him paint. And suddenly, I was overcome by a deep emotion . . . More, I was enlightened. Boudin truly initiated me. From that moment on, my way was clear, my destiny decreed. I would be a painter, come what may. And, as it turned out, my parents were dead set against it.*[7] From his other recollections in later life we equally learn only superficial facts about the artistic 'conversion' of the pupil when confronted with Boudin's example: *I watched more attentively, and then it was as if a veil had been torn aside . . . I had grasped what painting could be.*[8] *It is to Eugène Boudin that I owe the fact that I became a painter.*[9]

On 28 January 1857 Monet's mother died and the father and sons moved into the Lecadres' house at 13 Rue Fontanelle. Oscar was now completely at the mercy of his father's stubbornness and lack of understanding. However, help was at hand in the person of his widowed aunt Madame Lecadre, who was the only one of his relations interested in art. She arranged private tuition for her nephew with some of the officially recognised painters in the town and put at his disposal her own studio, where she herself dabbled in painting. Since Jacques Lecadre's death in 1858 Adolphe Monet had managed the family business, while the aunt enjoyed a pension and a legacy, including a property in Sainte-Adresse, a seaside suburb of Le Havre, where Monet painted at various times later in his life.

Apparently it was only at the age of 17, after his mother's death, that Monet told his father that he wanted to be a painter. Perhaps it was once he had realised that he could not change his son's mind – and surely also to save money – that Monet the businessman set about the task of financing his son's art studies, for on 6 August 1858 he applied to the Le Havre Town Council for a grant for Oscar. He renewed the application on 21 March 1859 but it was eventually refused, on the curious grounds that his early fame as a caricaturist would be a hindrance to the applicant in undertaking any serious artistic studies.

At any rate at the age of 60 Monet made out that his father had from the start been rigidly against his studying art and reported the following dialogue between father and son: *'You shall not have a penny.' 'I shall get along without it.' Indeed I could get along without it. I had long since made my little pile. My caricatures had done it for me. In one day I had often executed seven or eight caricature-portraits. At 20 francs apiece I had made a lot of money and from the start entrusted my earnings to one of my aunts, keeping only paltry sums for pocket money. At 16 one feels rich with 2000 francs. From several art-lovers who were patrons of Boudin and acquainted with Monginot, Troyon and Armand Gautier, I obtained some letters of introduction and set out post-haste for Paris.*[10]

STUDENT YEARS

With his savings of 2000 francs Oscar did not wait any longer for a decision about the grant, but at the end of April or beginning of May 1859 went off to Paris, in his pocket, among other things, a letter of recommendation from his aunt to her friend the salon painter Armand Gautier (1825-1894). He was warmly received by Gautier, and also by the historical painter Charles Lhuillier, now well established in the capital, who had been a pupil of his art-teacher Ochard and two years later painted a full-length portrait of Monet in uniform. Subsequently Oscar sought out the most distinguished of the three artists recommended by the 'amateur artist' from home and perhaps also by Boudin – the Barbizon landscape and animal painter Constant Troyon (1810-1865). Troyon praised the treatment of light and arrangement of colours in the two still life paintings from Le Havre which the budding artist showed him, but advised him to be more careful with his execution. He, together with Charles Monginot (1825-1900), another Parisian painter to whom Monet had an introduction and who let him paint in his studio for a while, recommended him for basic instruction to the teaching studio of the then renowned historical painter Thomas Couture (1815-1879), from which such differing artists as Édouard Manet and Anselm Feuerbach had emerged. Strengthened in visual skill and knowledge through his work with Boudin, the 18-year old already knew what he did *not* want, because he declined the offer of Couture as a teacher, thereby causing difficulties with his father, who had just declared that he was prepared to give his son a monthly allowance if he attended the school of that academician.

Over 40 years later Monet recalled his first period as a student in Paris: *It took me some little time at first to decide on a course of action. I called on the artists to whom I had letters. I received from them excellent advice; I received also some very bad advice. Did not Troyon want me to enter the studio of Couture? Needless to say I firmly refused to do so. I admit*

'Claude Monet as a Chasseur d'Afrique,' by Charles-Marie Lhuillier, 1861.
Musée Marmottan, Paris

that this even cooled (temporarily at least) my esteem and admiration for Troyon. I began to see less and less of him and, eventually only sought the company of artists engaged in a quest. At this juncture I met Pissarro, who had at that time not dreamt of posing as a revolutionary, but was tranquilly working in Corot's style. He was an excellent model; I followed his example, but during my whole stay in Paris, which lasted for four years and during which I frequently visited Le Havre, I was governed by Boudin's advice and was firmly resolved to view nature in the round.[11]

Camille Pissarro (1830-1903), who became one of Monet's closest impressionist colleagues, met Oscar at the so-called Académie Suisse, which he chose in preference to Couture's studio. This institution on the Ile de la Cité offered students studio space and models, without giving them any guidance or keeping them to any specific artistic course. Shortly afterwards, Paul Cézanne (1839-1906) enrolled there, too. Monet thus spared himself much of the outdated course of instruction, such as making drawings from antique plaster casts and copying in museums, which the pupils of the state academy were required to follow and which often stifled talent rather than encouraged it. At the Académie Suisse he could start straightaway with drawing and painting from nature without that kind of academic delay and interference.

Around 1860 this ideal particularly appealed to the so-called realists, among them Gustave Courbet (1819-1877), and the Barbizon painters, who in 1840 had first appeared on the scene with pictures painted direct from nature, this stance being opposed to the ruling academic, intellectual style of painting (above all the historical pictures, which inundated the annual official Salon exhibitions). It was particularly these early plein-air painters whom the young Monet was now studying and admiring in Paris. In a letter of 3 June 1859, when he was still only 18 years old, he wrote to his mentor Boudin about his visit to that year's Salon where – apart from Troyon (with reservations) and Camille Corot (1796-1875) – his highest praise was for Charles-François Daubigny

(1817-1878) who, like the other two, belonged more or less to the Barbizon school. Here he had stumbled upon an important soul mate. Soon after, on one of his visits to Le Havre, he came across a small, dirty picture in his aunt's house – *Grape-Picking at Twilight with Crescent Moon* – which she gave to her enraptured nephew. When it was cleaned, Daubigny's signature could be seen on it. In a letter to Boudin of 20 February 1860 Monet wrote about some additional impressions he had brought away from the exhibition. He was now especially enthusing about the works of Courbet and of Eugène Delacroix (1798-1863) as well as those of the Barbizon painters Corot, Jules Dupré (1811-1889), Théodore Rousseau (1812-1867) and Jean-François Millet (1814-1875). This is in effect a roll-call of the most important French forerunners of the future Impressionist, Claude Monet.

The young painter did not only devote himself to his art studies, but with his friends – those *artists who were on a quest* – he enjoyed the bohemian life to which the cafés, beer halls and other haunts of Paris beckoned. The Brasserie Bavaroise at 9 Rue des Martyrs particularly attracted the young artistic crowd. Here they had lively discussions – mainly between the academics and the progressives – and held wild parties. Enjoying himself cost money. Once when he was in financial difficulties he thoughtlessly sold his newly acquired little Daubigny. There is something superficial and opportunist in such behaviour on the part of a teenage student. This is the first evidence of shallowness, or at least inconsistency, which we frequently meet with in the course of Monet's later life.

These carefree, youthful antics in Paris soon came to an end. At the age of 60 Monet remembered: *I had reached my 20th year and the hour for conscription was about to strike. I saw its approach without fear and so did my family. They had not forgiven me my flight; they had let me live as I chose during those four years, only because they thought they would catch me when the time came for me to do military service. They thought that once my wild oats were sown, I would tame down sufficiently to return home readily enough and turn at last to commerce. If I refused, they would stop my allowance and if I drew an unlucky number they would let me go. They made a mistake. The seven years of service that appalled so many were full of attraction for me. A friend who was in the regiment of the Chasseurs d'Afrique and who adored military life had communicated to me his enthusiasm and inspired me with his love of adventure. Nothing attracted me so much as the endless cavalcades under the burning sun, the* razzias, *the crackle of gunpowder, the sabre thrusts, the nights in the desert under a tent, and I replied to my father's ultimatum with a superb gesture of indifference. I drew an unlucky number. I succeeded, by personal insistence, in being drafted into an African regiment and started out. In Algeria I spent two really charming years. I was always seeing something new; in my moments of leisure I attempted to reproduce what I saw. You cannot imagine to what extent I increased my knowledge and how much my vision gained thereby. I did not quite realise it at first. The impressions of light and colour that I received did not to crystallise until later but they contained the germ of my future researches.* [12]

One has the feeling that he was trying to emphasise how right his decision and his conduct at the time had been, by simplifying and embellishing much of it. In reality it must have been a gamble – a sort of roulette game. In the hope of drawing a lucky number in the lottery for recruits, the 20-year old boldly defied his father, who wanted him to go into business, for nothing had meanwhile become so important to him as learning to become a painter. The low number which the young man eventually drew condemned him to seven years' military service – a positively inhumanly long time to modern thinking. A young painter in the middle of his studies must have been shattered at such a prospect, but pride forbade Monet to admit it, even 40 years later. He wasted not a word on his father's undoubtedly hurtful refusal to buy his discharge for 2500 francs – an option which was legal and customary at the time not only in France, and which of course favoured well-to-do families. Adolphe Monet said he was only prepared to pay this sum if his son abandoned his art studies and entered on a business career. Even his art-loving aunt's influence had no effect. The intention was clearly to teach the headstrong youngster a lesson. But he, not unskilled in defending himself, took the wind out of his father's sails by pretending indifference and even enthusiasm for military life, perhaps in the hope that his father would give in at the last moment, if he did actually recognise that his son was completely determined. But that was not what actually happened.

On 29 April 1861 Oscar-Claude Monet was called up in Le Havre. The regimental records say that the recruit was 1.65 m tall and had brown eyes and brown hair. The full-length portrait painted that year by his older colleague Charles Lhuillier shows the picturesquely uniformed recruit in dark boots and wide red breeches under a blue-black frock-coat, on his head a red cap with a dark-blue visor. There is a photograph of the 20-year old Monet in civilian clothes in which, in contrast to Lhuillier's slightly later portrait, he has a full head of dark hair and a hint of a moustache and beard. Apart from some portraits painted a little later by artist friends, Monet's sensitive, vulnerable face looks out at us in this early period only; later his features were increasingly hidden behind a luxuriant growth of beard.

On 10 January 1861 Monet joined his regiment, stationed on the outskirts of Algiers, as a cavalryman, second class. *Being in uniform wasn't too bad. ... The officers took advantage of my talents a great deal, and that earned me some favours.*[13] From this comment, made when he was 73, it would seem that the budding artist was drawing or painting his seniors' portraits, but we know of none of them. In his free time he may also have had made sketches of the surrounding countryside, but the young recruit was definitely not particularly prolific during his military training, and to date no pictures of Africa have come to light.

Claude Monet in his twenties

After about nine months he contracted typhus and spent two months recuperating in Algeria. He was then granted six months convalescent leave, which he was allowed to spend at home. *They sent me home to recuperate. I spent six months of convalescence drawing and painting with redoubled energy. Seeing me persisting like this, weak as I was with fever, my father became convinced that no determination on his part could curb me and no ordeal would get the better of so determined a vocation, and as much for the sake of peace as from fear of losing me, for the doctor had led him to expect this, should I return to Africa, he decided towards the end of my furlough to buy me out.*[14] Writing when he was 60, Monet was mistaken in one respect: in fact it was not his father, but his aunt, who paid the 3000 francs needed to release him from the remaining six years at 500 francs a year, when he had barely recovered his health. She therefore paid more than the 2500 francs which would have excused him from ever being called up. In the event he served for barely a year, which did not excessively upset his artistic plans.

When he took up painting again during his convalescent leave in the summer of 1862, Monet made the acquaintance of the Dutch painter Johan-Barthold Jongkind (1819-1891), who frequently worked on the Normandy coast and some of whose pictures he already knew. Like Boudin, Jongkind liked to paint the sea and views of the shore, harbours and ships around Le Havre, but also the Seine in Paris. These two artists, of about the same age, were very similar in their spontaneous, unconventional method of plein-air painting and both were influenced by the older Barbizon painters. They may well have met that year, possibly introduced by Monet himself, who had met Jongkind by chance through an Englishman who had watched him painting out-of-doors. The somewhat eccentric Jongkind, who had a weakness for alcohol, lived and painted as a recluse and was hardly noticed by patrons of art. Monet recalled: *He asked to see my sketches, invited me to come and work with him, explained to me the why and wherefore of his style and thereby completed the teaching that I had already received from Boudin. From that time on he was my real master and it was to him that I owed the final education of my eye. I frequently saw him again in Paris. My painting, need I say, gained by it. I made rapid progress.*[15]

One almost gets the impression that Monet played his two similar, teachers off against each other, to Jongkind's advantage, but nevertheless Boudin was probably the more important to him as a teacher, for he was the first to take Monet the caricaturist under his wing, guide him into landscape painting and teach him a new way of looking at things. Although Boudin and Jongkind painted similar subjects in similar ways, they each had their own distinguishing style and both were equally accomplished.

With her classical leanings, Monet's aunt was uneasy about the artistic company he kept and the work he produced as a result. In 1862 she wrote to Armand Gautier about her headstrong nephew: 'His sketches are always rough drafts, like those you have seen; but when he wants to complete something, to produce a picture, they turn into appalling daubs before which he preens himself and finds idiots to congratulate him. He pays no attention to my remarks. I am not up to his level, so I now keep the most profound silence.'[16]

By 'idiots' she undoubtedly meant Boudin and Jongkind. After she met the unconventional, somewhat paranoid Jongkind personally, astonishingly enough she described him as 'a very great artist and above all a very good-natured fellow.'[17] Nevertheless she was determined to guide her nephew's further artistic training into a more reliable, that is academic, path. Auguste Toulmouche (1829-1890), a Parisian salon painter who was also dubbed a 'boudoir painter', had recently married into the family and was chosen by her as Oscar-Claude's mentor. Adolphe Monet also made any future financial support for his son dependant upon an 'academic' injunction, which he had to accept. In 1900 Monet recalled his father's stipulations: *'But it is well understood,' he said to me, 'that this time you are going to work in dead earnest. I wish to see you in an* atelier, *under the discipline of a well-known master. If you resume your independence, I will stop your allowance without more ado. Is it a bargain?' This arrangement did not more than half suit me, but I felt that it was necessary not to oppose my father when he for once entered into my plans. I accepted. It was agreed that in Paris the painter Toulmouche, who had just married one of my cousins, would be my artistic tutor, to guide me and furnish regular reports of my labours. I landed one fine morning at Toulmouche's with a stock of studies which he declared pleased him very much. 'You have a future,' he said, 'but you must direct your efforts in some given channel. You shall enter the studio of Gleyre. He is the staid and wise master that you need.'*[18]

The decision in favour of the academician Charles Gleyre (1806-1875) was certainly made in consultation with the Monet-Lecadre family, but Monet was anything but enthusiastic about the choice: *Grumbling, I put up my easel in the studio full of pupils, over which this celebrated artist presided. For the first week I worked there most conscientiously and with as much application as spirit made from the living model a nude study which Gleyre corrected on the Monday. The following week, he came over to me, sat down and, planted solidly on my chair, looked attentively at my work. Then – I can see him yet – he turned round and leaning his grave head to one side with a satisfied air, said to me: 'Not bad! Not bad at all, what you have done here, but it is too much in the character of the model. You have before you a short, thickset man and you paint him short and thickset; he has enormous feet, you render them as they are. All that is very ugly. I want you to remember, young man, that when one creates a figure, one should always think of the antique. Nature, my friend, is all right as an element of study but it offers no interest. Style, you see, style is everything.' I saw it all. Truth, life, nature, all that moved me, all that constituted in my eyes the very essence and the only raison d'être of art, did not exist for this man. I no longer wished to remain under him. I felt that I was not born to begin over again in his wake the* Illusions Perdues *and other kindred bores. Therefore, why persist? I nevertheless waited several weeks. In order not to exasperate my family, I continued to appear regularly at the studio, remaining only just long enough to execute a rough sketch from the model and to be present at inspection, then I slipped away. Moreover, in the studio I had found congenial companions, far from commonplace people. They were Renoir and Sisley, whom I was never thereafter to lose sight of, and Bazille, who immediately became my friend and who would have become famous had he lived. None of them manifested, any more than I did, the least enthusiasm for a mode of teaching that antagonised both their logic and their temperament. I forthwith preached rebellion to them. The exodus being decided on, we left, Bazille and I taking a studio together.*[19]

The fellow-students of about his age whom Monet met in Gleyre's academic studio, together with Pissarro whom he already knew from the Académie Suisse, embodied the actual nucleus of the French Impressionist group which later became internationally famous – Auguste Renoir (1841-1919), Frédéric Bazille (1841-1870) and Alfred Sisley (1839-1899), the Paris-born son of English parents, whose style later approached most closely to that of Monet.

In a conversation in 1914, Monet recalled the first steps which these friends eventually took together: *I honestly tried to work under him {Gleyre}. After a month I said to myself: 'What they do here is stupid.' Renoir and Sisley were my studio mates and I took them with me. I said: 'Let's go and paint out-of-doors.' But when my parents found out that I had left the atelier that Toulmouche had introduced me to, it was quite simple: they cut me off. Things were hard after that . . . My friends and I lived solely from the sale of our paintings. Needless to say, these sales were not always sufficient. I exhibited for the first time in the Salon of 1863 with two paintings, two seascapes,* Sainte-Adresse *and* Honfleur. *They were well placed and quite well received. The next year I sent in* The Woman with the Green Dress. *It was a great success and through it I met Manet.*[20]

Although they were rebelling against the academic, publicly appreciated and promoted art annually presented at the Salon, the only important major exhibition in Paris, the young painters considered that participating in this display of establishment pictures was the basic prerequisite for a successful career. Paul Cézanne and the somewhat older Éduard Manet (1832-1883), who both painted in impressionistic style for a while later on, struggled more obstinately and longer than the actual Impressionists to achieve popular recognition through acceptance by the Salon. Almost all these young painters – mostly from middle-class backgrounds – were on the one hand trying to justify to their families their choice of profession through popular success, while on the other hand their upbringing gave them a deep-seated desire for worldly honours. At the age of 73 Monet recalled: *Renoir, Sisley, Pissarro, Bazille and I – we were some of those bound by a common artistic direction. As long as we sent our work in to the Salon individually, we still had a chance of being shown. But once we exhibited privately as a group, we were labelled a 'gang' and turned down regularly. The judges didn't hesitate to give the reason behind their implacable ostracism: 'They're a gang with pretensions to a new and revolutionary art. A few are undeniably talented. If we seal their union with our approval, if we appear to attribute some value to their collective effort . . . it will mean the end of great art and of tradition.'*[21]

It is clear from this retrospective statement why the Impressionists experienced such difficulty in establishing themselves artistically in the 1860s and through into the 1870s. The representatives or promoters of academic art who headed the statutory institutions such as the State Academy of Arts, the Salon exhibitions, the Louvre and other museums were understandably concerned for their positions if a different, innovative type of painting were to find recognition. The ruling traditional camp was extremely successful for years in keeping the young painters away from state patronage by every imaginable means. The jury of the Salon was overwhelmingly stocked with conservative artists who, purely out of a sense of self-preservation, rejected and suppressed these aspiring painters. The official museums bought those academic works which had been successful in the Salon and the majority of the newspaper critics, led by the influential Albert Wolff of *Figaro,* judged according to conservative taste. This therefore created a cartel of established artists to secure and protect their property. By dubbing the young painters artistic revolutionaries, they implied that their art was politically dangerous. Tolerance of artistic deviation could even have been interpreted as an invitation to political liberalism. Napoleon III's regime might possibly have felt itself endangered by this undisciplined new painting.

So long as they were not identified as an organised 'league', individual young painters did actually succeed in getting into the Salon in the 1860s with a few works which were certainly not overwhelmingly revolutionary. After having two pictures accepted by the Salon in 1865 and then another one in 1866, the only work Monet submitted in 1867 was refused and in 1868 just one out of two was accepted. In the following two years the jury rejected all his submissions.[22]

The group of friends who had fled from Gleyre's studio followed up what they had decided to do when they recognised the fruitlessness of the academic instruction on offer: they painted en plein air, in the countryside. As they were mainly following the example of the Barbizon masters, it is not surprising that they chose as the scene for their painting the Forest of Fontainebleau, which lies to the south of Paris with Barbizon on its border. Barbizon was already overrun, so Monet, Renoir, Bazille and Sisley often took separate lodgings for long periods in the Cheval Blanc in the neighbouring village of Chailly-en-Bière, from which they set off daily for their chosen sites. They may possibly have met there some of the older Barbizon painters or other realists, such as Courbet.

In those years Monet was painting not only in Paris and the Forest of Fontainebleau, but also on the coast near Le Havre on his regular visits home, meeting up there with Boudin and Jongkind, both of whom he occasionally saw in Paris as well. In 1862 he signed a very academic hunting still life 'O. Monet', but from the following year started signing all his pictures 'C. Monet' or 'Claude Monet'. Just as Vincent van Gogh later dropped his surname from his signature to mark his alienation from an unsympathetic family, so Monet's changing his first name at the age of 22 can be seen as a psychological move. Now that his father had rejected his art and was no longer paying for his son's studies, Monet dropped the first name which had been used by his family in Le Havre.

Together with Bazille, his fellow-student from a well-to-do family in the southern town of Montpellier, who was also studying medicine (ultimately without success), Monet took a boat from Paris through Rouen to Le Havre in the summer of 1864. At Honfleur on the Normandy coast they found seascapes and views of the hinterland to paint. After Bazille had gone home, Monet - now painting with Boudin and Jongkind – wrote to him: *Nature is beginning to look lovely, more colourful and varied; it is remarkable and I think I shall stay in Honfleur for a while longer. I shall not have the courage to leave again. We went to Trouville several times, it is wonderful and I have promised myself to go back there next year and also to Etretat.*[23]

Renewed tensions between him and his father reached a climax when he was virtually thrown out of the house. At the end of October Monet commented on the situation in a letter to Bazille: *I am even afraid that I shan't get any more money.*[24] Presumably the quarrel was mainly over Monet's refusal to continue studying with Gleyre. For several years thereafter the young painter was almost perpetually in severe financial straits, and Bazille frequently had to help him out with loans. At the end of 1864 Bazille rented a spacious studio at 6 Rue de Furstemberg in Paris, close to the studio where Delacroix had worked until his death in 1863, and allowed Monet, who lived in a room in a distant part of town, to share it.

Now that he could no longer count on his father's support, Monet found that, even more than before, he had to rely on his own talents to achieve success and recognition. In the following years his activities seem to have followed a rigorously planned course. He was already at least partially successful in his annual attempts to be accepted by the Salon. In 1863 in the *Salon des Refusés* – the exhibition of works rejected by the Salon jury, which played a significant part in the history of Impressionism – Monet saw Édouard Manet's *Déjeuner sur l'Herbe,* which roused a great, hypocritical scandal, because it depicted a naked woman sitting between men in modern street clothes. It was less the realistic, almost photographic, studio picture than the 'shameless' subject which had enraged a public accustomed to paintings of embellished historical or mythological events. After his two Normandy seascapes had been accepted by the Salon in 1865, Monet now attacked an ambitious project for the following year's Salon: a painting more than six metres wide, also entitled *Déjeuner sur l'Herbe (Luncheon on the Grass).* His objective was to paint a composition with life-size figures in the open air, that is, in the natural sunlight specific to a time of day and year. Nothing of the sort had existed for ages and he doubtless wanted it to attract attention and make him famous. In it Monet was already obsessively concerned – as he was throughout his artistic life – with capturing what he called 'instantaneousness' (*instantanéité*). *I can only think of my picture,* he wrote at the time, *if it isn't a success, I'll probably go mad.*[25] Even in later years he often expressed himself in such theatrical terms when grappling with creative difficulties.

After completing the preliminary studies, he tackled the huge canvas. For the seven men and six women grouped around a picnic cloth spread out in a woodland clearing he used as models Bazille and his mistress and future wife, Camille Doncieux. In order to be able to paint the upper parts of the massively high canvas, Monet dug a ditch into which he could lower the picture.

'The wounded Claude Monet at the Hotel du Lion d'Or in Chailly-en-Biere,'
by Frédéric Bazille, 1865. Musée d'Orsay, Paris

Varied, confusing, positive and negative comments on his project
came, among others, from Courbet, who for a while had been
associating with Monet and his friends, but also from Boudin,
who had deliberately restricted himself to smaller pictures and who
wrote to his brother about this failed venture: 'Monet has finished
his enormous jam sandwich, which has taken all his strength.'[26]

In the autumn Monet injured his leg and for a while had to stay
in bed in Chailly. His friend Bazille invented a contraption to cool
the leg with a constant trickle of water and kept him company while
he was laid up by painting him in this tragicomic situation. Finally
the onset of winter drove them back to Paris, where Monet's attempts
to complete his gigantic picture were unsuccessful. This ill-fated
work finally served as a pledge for a creditor who kept it in a damp
place, so that when years later the painter redeemed it, it was stained
with mildew in several places and its creator had to cut it into two
pieces, in which form it still exists. In his old age Monet enjoyed
telling visitors the sad story of this ambitious youthful project.

Claude Monet
1866

He had nothing suitable as a substitute available for the 1866 Salon. He therefore painted, apparently in just four days, the life-size, full-length portrait of *Camille, or the Woman with a green Dress,* 1866, Kunsthalle, Bremen, (on facing page); the complete opposite to what he had planned with the *Luncheon on the Grass.* It was an almost too precisely painted studio portrait which, in spite of its qualities, approached suspiciously close to the items generally acceptable to the Salon. It is therefore not surprising that this work, together with a Fontainebleau landscape, was accepted by the jury and it had a great success. This time Monet certainly negotiated a fee and was officially paid.

Following on his success at the Salon, he immediately embarked on another ambitious project: a figure composition 2.5 metres high entitled *Women in the Garden,* also painted en plein air but considerably smaller than the *Luncheon on the Grass.* However, it was voted out. To help his friend financially, Bazille bought it for the relatively high sum of 2500 francs, which he paid to Monet in small monthly instalments. After Bazille's early death, his parents exchanged with Édouard Manet a portrait of their son painted by Renoir against this large canvas of Monet's. Following on another exchange, the picture eventually returned to its painter and in 1921 was bought by the Louvre. The 20-year old Camille, who came from a modest background, was most probably the model for all four women in this painting. A close relationship had meanwhile developed between her and Monet, who was her senior by six years.

After his success with *Camille or the Woman with a green Dress* at the 1866 Salon (Monet sold several paintings for 800 francs, including a smaller reproduction of the Camille picture), his aunt decided to continue supporting her unruly but clearly talented nephew financially but not to settle his debts. In April Monet rented a cottage for himself and Camille at Ville d'Avray near Sèvres, and painted *Women in the Garden* nearby. But they did not stay there long; by the summer new debts forced Monet to flee, leaving pictures and other possessions behind. He went to Honfleur, to paint an ambitious view of the harbour for the next year's Salon which, however, rejected it, together with *Women in the Garden*. This large plein-air composition was then exhibited for a time in the window of the Paris paint-dealer Latouche, where it attracted attention.

Early in 1867 Monet and Camille went to live in Bazille's studio at 20 Rue Visconti, where Renoir had also found refuge. In May Monet painted three remarkable views of Paris seen from the Louvre and reported on them to Bazille: *Renoir and I are continuing to work on our scenes of Paris.*[27] These three views were rejected by the Salon jury in 1869 and then again displayed by Latouche.

After his failure at the 1867 Salon Monet found himself once again in financial straits. His father imposed a new condition on further material support: Oscar was to give up his mistress (who was clearly not socially acceptable). Camille was pregnant and Monet found himself compelled to appear to accede to his father's demand, which was all the more hypocritical because in 1860 Adolphe had fathered an illegitimate daughter on his maid. On 10 June he went to Le Havre to throw himself virtually on the mercy of his relatives, because he needed money from both his father and his aunt to support his future family. On 8 August, while he was still away, Camille gave birth to their son Jean. At the time Monet was living in his aunt's country house in Sainte-Adresse, apparently reconciled with his family and busy painting seascapes. As he was only receiving his living expenses, he wrote urgent letters to Bazille. His worries over the forthcoming birth of his child led him to report on actual or deliberately dramatised health problems. On 3 July he wrote to his friend: *I am in great trouble; just think, I am losing my sight, after half an hour's work I can hardly see any more.* In a further letter dated 20 August he was pressing his friend, who had obviously not yet sent him any money: *It is usual to think about one's friends' troubles; therefore I do not believe in your friendship any more. I need you more than ever, you know why and it makes me ill. If you do not answer me, it is all over between us. You can be sure that I should never write to you again.*[28] Later on he again demonstrated an almost tactless and shameless obstinacy resulting from artistic egotism – an unappealing and contradictory trait in Monet's character, seeing that he was always capable of sensitivity and ready to help other people.

Having only visited Camille and the new baby on short visits to Paris, at the onset of winter Monet rented a room in the Batignolles district of the city. Bazille, with whom he was apparently still on good terms, offered him the use of his nearby studio and even helped his friend to sell a still life. In January and February Monet was back in Le Havre, working on a picture of the mole in winter, which he intended for the next year's Salon. Unlike other plein-air painters, he worked through the cold season directly in front of his landscapes. What that cost him all his life long we can judge from a contemporary who watched him painting a winter scene: 'We found a foot-warmer, then an easel and then a man huddled in three overcoats, with gloves on his hands and a half-frozen face. This was Monet, working on a snow-study. Art has brave soldiers who lack nothing for courage.'[29]

To the end of his life Monet vacillated between phases of contentment and harmony, and of despair and depression. Reading his letters to members of his family or to friends, one cannot escape the impression that he liked to exaggerate and embroider gloomy situations and emotions, because he wanted something from the addressee – material or moral support. After the Salon had rejected both his submissions for 1868, he wrote that spring to Bazille: *My painting is not going well and I have finally given up any thought of becoming famous. I am experiencing the greatest failure. I have not actually achieved anything whatever since I left you. I have become utterly lazy, everything seems boring as soon as I try to work. I am in a black mood. To add to this I am penniless. It is all disappointments, insults, hopes and again disappointments, my friend... At least I managed to sell something, which didn't bring in much, but perhaps is a good sign for the future, although I don't believe in that any more.* At the end of June he wrote to him again from Bennecourt on the Seine: *I was definitely born under a bad star. I have just been thrown out of the inn, as naked as a worm. I have found a shelter for Camille and my poor little Jean in the country for a few days . . . My family won't do anything more for me. I therefore don't know where I shall lay my head tomorrow. Your most agonised friend, Claude Monet. P.S. I was so distraught that I was silly enough to throw myself into the water. Fortunately without any bad effect.*[30] This has long been regarded as an impulsive, desperate suicide attempt, but one is entitled to entertain doubts: it might well have been another, this time particularly dramatic, attempt to blackmail Bazille. Monet was a good swimmer and would have found it difficult to drown in the warm summer waters of this tributary of the Seine.

Shortly before this occurrence his professional situation improved. At the end of June, having settled Camille and Jean in nearby Fécamp, Monet went to Le Havre, where he entered five pictures in the newly opened International Seafaring Exhibition and was even awarded a silver medal. But his exhibits were seized by his creditors. A new, rich client, Louis-Joachim Gaudibert, eventually redeemed the works and commissioned Monet to paint a portrait of his wife, which the painter – imitating his successful portrait of *Camille or the Woman with a Green Dress* – did in very agreeable circumstances while staying at Gaudibert's castle in the Ardennes. The portrait was somewhat coolly received by the subject's family and only the husband-patron showed any satisfaction; he then supported Monet by buying some more of his works. In spite of these strokes of luck Monet again wrote bitterly to Bazille at the end of October: *Painting is no good, and I have definitely given up all hopes of glory.*[31] A few years later it must have occurred to Monet that his vision of success and the strategies he was employing were false and were actually preventing him from developing his own individual artistic vision. As with other painters, only trial by failure led him to find himself.

In spite of his blackmailing letters, towards the end of 1868 Monet was enjoying quite a happy time with Camille and Jean in Etretat, a resort on the Channel coast renowned for its precipitous coastline, whose combination of the natural elements of sky, sea and cliffs had inspired the creativity of older painters such as Courbet. Monet also returned to it again and again and to other prosperous bathing resorts around Le Havre. In December he wrote a conciliatory letter to Bazille, who was godfather to his little son: *I am surrounded here with everything I love. I spend my time in the open air on the shingle when it is fine or when the fishing boats are going out; or in the country which is so beautiful here, even lovelier in winter than in summer. And naturally I am working all the time and I believe I shall produce something of value this year. And then in the evening, my dear friend, I find in my little house a good fire and a good little family. Thanks to that gentleman from Le Havre who has come to my aid {Gaudibert}, I am enjoying the most perfect tranquillity, free from drudgery. So my wish would be to stay forever like this in such a restful corner of nature. So I do not envy you being in Paris. Honestly, I do not believe I could work fruitfully in such surroundings . . . Do you not believe that nature can even do better? I am convinced of it and anyhow I always thought I painted better in such conditions. One is too preoccupied with what one sees and hears in Paris, however resolute one might be. And my work here has at least the merit of not being like anyone else's, because it is simply the impression of what I myself have felt entirely on my own. The more I see the more I regret how little I know: that is what bothers me most. The further I go, the more clearly I realise that one never dares to express what one experiences. It is strange . . .*[32] He seemed to be suppressing his naked obsession with his career and to be thinking about true artistic values, which had primarily little to do with superficial matters such as transient success at exhibitions or sales. He had chosen the right path.

This new consciousness was reflected in the following year in positive artistic events. For the Salon Monet was working on a winter scene 1.3 metres wide, *The Magpie*, one of his first real masterpieces, doubtless mostly painted out-of-doors in the cold and snow. He submitted it and an equally large seascape to the 1869 Salon, but both works were rejected. Instead of falling back into a black mood over this new failure, this time Monet took the initiative: once again he presented the paint-dealer Latouche, who in January had displayed one of his views of Paris seen from the Louvre in his shop-window, with a large-scale seascape he had painted in the summer of 1867, *The Garden at Sainte-Adresse* (New York), and it also attracted attention.

He then moved with his little family to the village of Saint-Michel, which lay near the left bank of the Seine between Louveciennes and Bougival, where he spent a good and fruitful summer painting; this time not even his renewed money problems were a serious obstacle. Renoir, who was living in nearby Voisins, helped his neighbour with food, which he begged or 'borrowed' from his parents. On 9 August 1869 Monet reported in a letter to Bazille: *Renoir brings us bread to stop us starving. For a week we have had no bread, no fire and no light, it is appalling.*[33] Renoir, who was himself unsuccessful and under pressure materially, told Bazille: 'I'm at my parents' house, and am always round at Monet's, where things are, incidentally, pretty bad. Some days they don't eat at all. Still, I'm not unhappy because, for painting, Monet is good company.'[34]

In fact the two friends painted some novel, avant-garde landscapes on the banks of the Seine, which were fundamentally the first true Impressionist works of all. Into the following year Monet continued to paint Seine landscapes in and around Bougival and street scenes in Louveciennes, where Pissarro (also living there in penury), sometimes worked on the same subjects at his side. On 25 September 1869 Monet wrote another begging letter to Bazille: *This year I shall be the only one to have achieved nothing. This makes me rage against everyone. I am envious, angry and distraught. If I could work, everything would be all right. You say neither 50 nor 100 francs would get me out of this mess. That may be so, but in that case there is nothing for me to do but to run my head against the wall, because I have no hope of any unexpected windfall.*[35]

In the spring of 1870 the two pictures Monet submitted to the Salon – *La Grenouillère* and the *Luncheon* – were both rejected. Corot and Daubigny, who were both members of the jury, had spoken in his favour but were outvoted, whereupon they resigned their honorary positions. In spite of this new blow – perhaps also on account of the threat of war with Prussia – Monet now decided to marry Camille. On 28 June the wedding took place in Paris with Courbet as one of the witnesses. In the course of the necessary formalities Monet was questioned about his military background and realised that the authorities now regarded him as a potential reservist.

On 7 July his aunt died at Sainte-Adresse. During the summer the couple and their child stayed at the Hotel Tivoli in Trouville and spent the days on the beach with the Boudins. On the eve of war the two painters were celebrating this happy time in their drawings and paintings. In his old age Boudin recalled this period in a letter to Monet: 'I can still see you with that poor Camille in the Hôtel Tivoli. I have even kept a drawing I made that shows you on the beach... Little Jean is playing in the sand and his papa is sitting on the ground with a sketch-pad in his hand.'[36] When Prussia declared war on France on 19 July 1870, they felt quite safe in Trouville, but in September, when he could not settle the hotel bill and was also afraid of being called up, Monet decided to go to England.

EXILE AND SELF-DISCOVERY

Before he left for the coast with Camille and his son, Monet had sent a number of pictures from Bougival to Pissarro in nearby Louveciennes for safekeeping, fearing that they might be impounded to pay his debts. In or around October 1870 he arrived in England, leaving his wife and child to follow a little later. At first they lived at 11 Arundel Street and from January 1871 at Bath Place in the City. His friend Bazille, who had volunteered for military service, was killed at Beaune-la-Rolande on 28 November, at the age of only 30.

Before his departure Monet had paid a visit to his sick father in Le Havre but they parted acrimoniously. In London he learnt that, having married his mistress and acknowledged their illegitimate child Marie a few weeks before, Adolphe Monet had died on 17 January 1871. The war made it impossible for Monet to attend the funeral. In 1900 Monet recalled his time in London: *I suffered want. England did not care for our paintings. It was hard. By chance I ran across Daubigny, who had formerly shown some interest in me. He was then painting scenes of the Thames that pleased the English very much. He was moved by my distress. 'I see what you need,' he said. 'I am going to bring a dealer to you.' The next day I made the acquaintance of Mr Durand-Ruel. And Mr Durand-Ruel was our saviour.*[37] In another reminiscence he wrote: *In 1870 we fled to London. We – Pissarro, Boudin and I – frequently went to a café where all the French used to meet. Daubigny would sometimes drop by. He realised we were all spiritual brothers and wanted to see our painting. He then got very excited, very enthusiastic, and assured Pissarro and myself of his support.*[38]

The Parisian art-dealer Paul Durand-Ruel had also fled to London and founded a branch of his firm there. Loyal and dependable Daubigny recommended Monet to him in the following terms: 'Here is a man who will be better than any of us . . . Buy: I promise to take any [pictures] you can't sell and give you paintings of mine in exchange.'[39] In the long run Durand-Ruel did not regret his decision to handle Monet's affairs. In 1914 Monet paid tribute to his dealer's virtues: *From that moment on Durand-Ruel supported all of us. It was a heroic venture. Someone should study the role of this great dealer in the history of Impressionism.*[40] Durand-Ruel displayed one of Monet's pictures – a view of Trouville harbour – in his first London exhibition which opened on 10 December 1870, leading one to conclude that the painter took with him to England some, if not all, of the works he had done that summer.

Camille Pissarro had to leave behind in Louveciennes both his own pictures and those Monet had left with him. In his absence Prussian soldiers were quartered in his house and vandalised it, destroying a large number of works, particularly his own. He was living in Lower Norwood and went with Monet to visit museums and other places in the winter of 1870/71. In the London galleries they studied, among others, the works of Turner and Constable, which certainly had a strong influence on their own painting. In old age Monet tried hard to deny or play down this influence. He clearly regarded his own place in the history of art belittled by comparison with Turner: *The fatal comparison with Turner obviously leads to that and what would art criticism be without comparisons?*[41] Pissarro, too, later declared that the relationship between the two English artists and the Impressionists was a coincidence – a chance spiritual affinity, as he wrote to William Dewhurst in November 1902: ' . . . We also visited the museums [in London] . . . but we were struck chiefly by the landscape painters, who shared more in our aim with regard to plein air, light and fugitive effects.'[42]

Unlike in Louveciennes, in London Monet and Pissarro did not paint side by side but each on his own. Only seven paintings are known from the six months or so which Monet spent in London, among them two views of Hyde Park and four of the Thames. Their quality is nowhere near that of the first purely Impressionist works he had already painted in Bougival and Trouville. Perhaps he found it difficult to 'observe' in London and the cold season may also have been to blame for these products, which were slight not only in number.

Perhaps Monet first had to develop what he had experienced

and felt at that time in front of Turner's and Constable's pictures. After two of his paintings had been lent by Durand-Ruel for the International Exhibition in the South Kensington Museum in May, he left England with his wife and child to spend the summer in Holland. Here his output blossomed both in quantity and quality. On 2 June they arrived in Zaandam, a small town near Amsterdam, possibly on the recommendation of Jongkind or Daubigny. Its numerous canals and windmills, the abundance of water and the canopy of sky stretching over the flat countryside were ideal subjects for Monet the plein-air painter and by the autumn he had completed at least two dozen major pictures, which count among his very best works to date. He wrote to Pissarro the day he arrived: *Zaandam is particularly remarkable. One could paint here all one's life.*[43] Boudin, meeting Monet that autumn on his return to Paris, was enthusiastic about his pupil's new works. On 2 January 1872 he wrote about him: 'He brought back some very beautiful works from Holland and I believe he will hold one of the top places in our school of painting.'[44]

After being inspired by Turner and Constable in London, Monet was further stimulated by some other, earlier painters. On 22 July 1871 he visited the Trippenhuis (later the Rijksmuseum), where he studied Old Dutch masters such as Frans Hals and Rembrandt, and landscape painters like Jacob van Ruisdael and Jan van Goyen. He probably bought his first Japanese woodcuts in Amsterdam, where he stayed for a while from 2 October.

Although Camille was earning some money by giving private French lessons in Zaandam, Monet's own financial situation must have been improving considerably. Through Durand-Ruel's purchases, his legacy (though probably only a small one) from his father and Camille's dowry he could meet their daily needs for the first time. Around the middle of November he took a new flat near the Gare Saint-Lazare in Paris. Unlike other colleagues, who kept away for fear of being personally compromised, Monet and Boudin went to visit Courbet in prison, where he was serving a sentence for his part as a revolutionary in the Paris Commune. Although he had weaknesses, Monet showed an amazing amount of social courage in situations he considered important.

FROM ARGENTEUIL TO GIVERNY

Monet only stayed in Paris for a few weeks. Towards the end of 1871 he rented for 1000 francs a year a house in Argenteuil, which lies on the Seine ten kilometres northwest of Paris and at the time numbered about 8000 inhabitants. Because of its good railway connections (15 minutes from the capital) it had become a favourite resort with the Parisians. The riverside scenery was peopled with bathers, rowers and walkers and for the next years provided a wealth of material for Monet, as also for the fellow-painters who visited him there – Renoir, Sisley and even Manet. The two great bridges over the Seine, which had just been restored after war damage, particularly attracted him and from now on they kept appearing in his river scenes. The house which Manet found for them lay downstream from the railway station and from its windows Monet could see *everything that happened on the Seine, some 40 or 50 paces distant.*[45] He had a houseboat built, from which he could paint different subjects from unusual angles while floating on the river. In this he was emulating Daubigny, who some years before had made excursions from his home at Auvers in a painting boat on the river Oise.

The years of consolidation after the Franco-Prussian War brought a substantial improvement in Monet's finances. Having earned 12,100 francs for 38 paintings in 1872, he recorded 24,800 francs in 1873, as Durand-Ruel paid the same amount for 25 paintings as for the previous 38. So prices had risen. In the 1860s he had often given away his pictures for 50, 100 or 200 francs but now – according to the picture in question – could receive up to 500 per work and in one exceptional case as much as 2000. He could therefore pay a year's rent by selling two or three paintings.

However a general recession in 1874 caused the situation to deteriorate again. Durand-Ruel had to cut back and for a while was accepting no new pictures. At the end of 1873 Camille was paid 6000 francs from her inheritance on the death of her father and in the autumn of 1875 she gave a further 2000 to the paint-dealer Carpentier, to whom Monet owed money.

The years from 1872, in which various members of the group of painters met in Argenteuil to work, marked the real blossoming of Impressionism. In spite of their still shaky material circumstances Renoir, Sisley and above all Monet (also Pissarro in Pontoise and Auvers) were creating masterpieces in the new style, which for a long time had been a secret tip for just a few collectors and to which only one single serious art-dealer – Durand-Ruel – had yet committed himself. As since his return from England Monet had given up submitting works to the annual Salon and his and his friends' sporadic participation in regional exhibitions brought in no income worth the name, the young painters were pondering over alternatives. Finally at the end of 1873 they formed an alliance with the aim of organising a larger group exhibition in Paris in 1874. It was held from 15 April to 15 May in the former studios on the Boulevard des Capucines of the well-known photographer Nadar (which happened to be empty), and was met with overwhelming scorn and disapproval from the critics. One of Monet's pictures, a misty harbour view of Le Havre – *Impression, Sunrise* – gave rise to the derisive nickname 'impressionist', which all the painters (with the exception of Edgar Degas (1834-1917) who was violently opposed to it) greeted as an accolade.

Although Monet is now regarded as the leading Impressionist and in his own lifetime was also one of the driving artistic and organising forces of the group, he only took part in the first four exhibitions of the association – in 1874, 1876, 1877 and 1879. While for tactical motives and because of growing acrimony among members of the group he did not take part in the 1880 and 1881 Impressionist exhibitions, he did exhibit for the last time in the seventh in 1882. In the final exhibition in 1886 he took no part because he did not like some of the artists associated with it – Paul Gauguin, for example. Instead in 1879 and lastly in 1880 he successfully submitted occasional works to the Salon, which his friends held against him. Both opportunities for exhibiting put Monet – as also most of his Impressionist friends – in a dilemma: if one exhibited with the group on one's own responsibility, one risked financial failure and (worse still) the danger of being bracketed together by public and critics with the less gifted 'fellow-travellers' of the Impressionists. Also one gained less personal profile as a member of a stylistic movement than by exhibiting independently in the Salon, although it was admittedly still run on conservative lines. However, some skilful second-class painters were gradually jostling their way into the Salon – painters who, with surprising success, managed to apply some overlay of Impressionist style to the outdated themes of the Salon pictures. With such 'fellow-travellers' Monet did not want to be associated. Since 1883 he had come too far to need to avail himself of either of these alternative types of exhibition and from then on he mainly sent pictures to international exhibitions or mounted solo shows in Paris.[46]

In January 1874, before the first Impressionist exhibition opened, Monet went via Le Havre to Amsterdam to paint a dozen harbour and street scenes, already in the decidedly Impressionistic style he had developed since he settled in Argenteuil, where in October 1874 he moved to a house with a garden, for which he paid 1400 francs a year.

After the failure of their group exhibition in the spring, Monet and his fellow-painters tried to better their straitened circumstances caused by the economic situation by holding an auction in Maison Drouot in Paris in March 1875. Altogether 163 works by Berthe Morisot (a pupil of Manet's), Sisley, Renoir and Monet came under the hammer. The bidding was shamefully low; most of Monet's 20 pictures reached less than 200 francs apiece and only two went above 300. A few he had to buy back himself to save them from being sold for a song. Altogether 1875 was a disappointing year financially for him – a bitter setback, for by the end of the year his total income had only reached 9765 francs, significantly less than in the previous years.

Nevertheless by then he had acquired some new collectors, who bought pictures from him in the following years as well, even though for relatively low prices. For example, Jean-Baptiste Faure, a celebrated baritone at the Paris Opera, spent 4200 francs in 1874 on buying works by Monet. Another major collector, though not a very opulent one, was Victor Choquet, who acquired more paintings by Renoir and Cézanne than by Monet. In the spring of 1876 Monet painted several remarkable views of the Tuileries from Choquet's apartment in the Rue de Rivoli. Gustave Caillebotte (1848-1894), the wealthy son of a ship-builder who himself painted in a similar style to that of the Impressionists but has always been under-estimated, not only helped to organise group exhibitions for the painters of this new stylistic movement, but also over the years put together a remarkable and extensive collection of their works, the best of which are now in the Musée d'Orsay. Apart from Manet, whom Monet approached several times for financial help or loans during these years of renewed poverty, it was first and foremost Caillebotte who repeatedly lent money to the painters he admired or helped them by purchasing their works.

Another important collector had emerged in the past years, especially as a buyer of Monet's works at the 1875 Drouot auction. He was Ernest Hoschedé (1837-1891), the wealthy owner of a Paris store who speculated, among other things, in art. In 1876 he commissioned Monet to execute several large decorative paintings for his wife Alice's Castle at Rottembourg near Montgeron, for which (as he was insolvent) he mostly paid with goods from his shops. The name Hoschedé was to play an important, even fateful, role in Monet's later life. As a patron he was only useful to Monet for a short while, because in August of the following year he went bankrupt, doubtless on account of his risky speculations. When his collection went to auction in the summer of 1878, numerous works by Monet came under the hammer and were knocked down for extremely low prices. However, these events in no way damaged the good relationship between the Monets and the Hoschedés.

In 1876 Camille Monet fell seriously ill, probably as the result of a bungled abortion, and the birth of their second child, Michel, on 17 March 1878 completely undermined her health. When the family moved in August of that year from Argenteuil to Vétheuil, the now impoverished Hoschedés joined them. Alice Hoschedé, née Raingo, came from an upper-class family. She herself had six children – four daughters and two sons – and looked after the ailing Camille, little Jean and the newborn baby as well. It was clear that Monet's attachment to Alice went beyond mere friendship, even while Camille was alive, and it is not impossible that Monet was the father of Alice's last child, Jean-Pierre, who was born on a train when they were travelling to Biarritz.

From the previous six years, which Monet had mainly spent in Argenteuil, about 150 landscape paintings of the surrounding countryside exist and today rank among the masterpieces of Impressionism. Journeys to Normandy (to his beloved Channel coast and to Rouen) as well as periods in Holland in 1874 and at Rottembourg Castle, brought variety into his plein-air landscapes and cityscapes, including several views of Paris. In 1877 he set up his easel in the Gare Saint-Lazare and painted a dozen pictures of the station hall with its metal rails and steaming locomotives. Eventually Argenteuil and its surroundings had no new subjects to offer him and so it became necessary to move house.

From March the family were living in Paris, where Monet was

painting on the banks of the Seine and on 30 June portrayed the city decorated with bunting to celebrate the National Day, but in August 1878 he again went on his travels, which this time led him to Vétheuil, a small town on the Seine about 60 kilometres northwest of Paris, where he at once began painting with enthusiasm. On 1 September he wrote: *I have set up my tent on the bank of the Seine at Vétheuil, in enchanting surroundings.*[47] Vétheuil, which lies on a bend in the river, its sister-town Lavacourt on the other bank and the countryside around offered the principal subjects for Monet's landscape paintings over the next years. The Monets first took lodgings with the Hoschedés in a cottage on the road to Mantes but by the end of the year they had all moved into a more spacious house at the other end of the town on the road to La Roche-Guyon. In Paris Monet kept a studio at 20 Rue de Ventimille to store his works and as a pied-à-terre for his regular visits to the capital to sell his pictures and attend to other business.

In 1877 Monet earned 15,000 francs – a definite, if slow, upward trend, having sold a good number of pictures, though for very low prices. In spite of this income he still owed money and was fearful that some of his pictures might be seized in settlement of these debts. He was both miserly and spendthrift. His financial situation was still critical, partly because of the recession but also because of his higher living standard, and from the middle of the 1870s he was once again writing begging letters to friends, acquaintances and collectors. They sound a touch too dramatic or even like ultimatums. In the winter of 1876/77 he turned to the writer Émile Zola: *Could you and would you do me a great favour? If by tomorrow evening, Tuesday, I have not paid the sum of 600 francs, all our furniture and everything I own will be sold and we ourselves will be turned out onto the street. I have not a penny to put towards this sum. Not one of the sales I counted on has materialised yet. So in one last attempt I am turning to you . . .*[48] We do not know whether or not Zola came to his aid.

In June 1877 Monet wrote to his doctor Georges de Bellio, a

collector: *I am desperately unlucky; my possessions are being seized at the very moment when I hoped to put my affairs in order. If I find myself in the street without any resources, I shall just have to look for a job. That would be a terrible blow for me. I cannot think of it and am risking one last attempt. I could save the situation with 500 francs . . . I have about 25 pictures left. I will give them to you for that amount. If you do this, you would help me . . .*[49] But Monet did not have to sell off his works quite so cheaply. De Bellio bought 'only' ten pictures from him, paying the derisory price of 100 francs each.

At the end of December 1878 he turned once more in despair to de Bellio: *I am not a beginner any more and it is awful at my age to be in such a position, always begging and pestering buyers. At this time of year I feel my misfortune doubly, because '79 is beginning, as this year ends, in my complete dejection, especially on account of my loved ones, as I can't buy them even the smallest present.* He was particularly worried about Camille, whose state of health had greatly deteriorated. In the following months he wrote more letters to other friends and collectors, describing his situation in gloomy terms. On 10 March 1879 he was again writing to de Bellio: *I am totally disgusted and worn down by the life I have had to live for so long. If this is all a man of my age has achieved, there is nothing more to hope for. Unhappy we are and unhappy we shall remain. Every day brings its worries and with every day come new difficulties from which we cannot extricate ourselves. I am therefore giving up the struggle and any hopes; in these conditions I have no more strength to work. I gather that my friends are preparing a new exhibition this year; I am declining to participate because I have nothing worth exhibiting.*[50] Compared with the letters which Vincent van Gogh (1853-1890), who embarked on his artistic career at the same time as Monet, wrote to his brother, also showing that he was in financial straits, the latter's laments and cries for help often sound rather rhetorical and overdone; they are designed to arouse pity in the potential benefactor. In spite of what he wrote to de Bellio, Monet was certainly not going to ignore the

Impressionist exhibition of 1879, and in fact contributed to it 30 pictures he valued.

However, low income, Camille's serious illness and even some well-wishers' adverse criticism of his newer pictures plunged him into a personal and artistic crisis. After almost two decades of privations, Monet had to ask himself how much longer he could keep going as a painter and whether there was any sense in it all. Like van Gogh, who was also impoverished but on the brink of recognition at the time of his early death, Monet could not know that he only had to endure one last bad year before reaching the turning-point on the road to success.

On 5 September 1879 Camille died in Vétheuil at the age of only 33. Many years later Monet confided to his old friend Georges Clemenceau how he had reacted to the sight of his wife's dead body: *One day, finding myself at the bedside of a dead woman, who had been and always was very dear to me, I surprised myself, my eyes fixed on her tragic features, in the act of tracing mechanically the subtle succession of shades of colouring which death had laid over the motionless face. Blues, yellows and greys, or whatever? So that's what I had come to! The desire to reproduce a last image of her who had left us forever was quite natural. Yet even before the idea came to me of fixing those features to which I was so deeply attached, I was already automatically, organically shaken by the impact of her colouring and the reflections so engrossed me against my will in an unconscious action, returning to the daily course of my life. Like an animal, turning a millwheel. Pity me, my friend.*[51] His habit as an artist of studying reflections of light and colour led Monet to bid farewell to his wife in his own way; the painting which records this moment depicts Camille as Ophelia caught at the moment of drowning, floating in reddish, yellow and blue effects of light. Although he was later ashamed of giving way to his obsession with painting when faced with death, it should be regarded as a wholly honourable work of art and an impressive act of mourning.

Three weeks after Camille's death Monet wrote to Pissarro: *I*

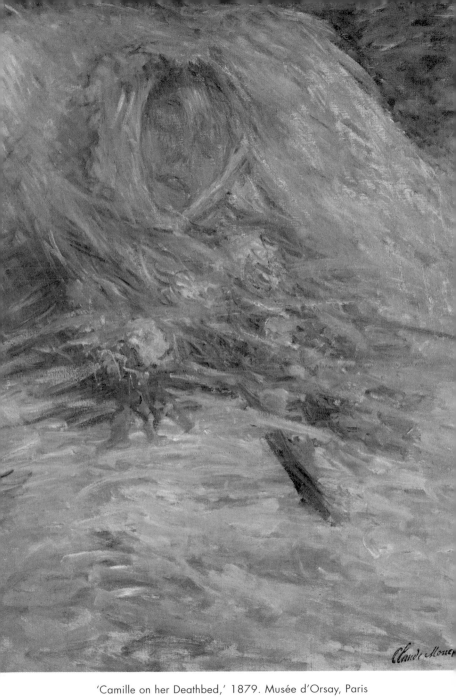

'Camille on her Deathbed,' 1879. Musée d'Orsay, Paris

am depressed, because I do not know how to sort myself out nor how to organise my life with my two children. Pity me, for I am much to be pitied.[52] The dead woman survives to the present day primarily through her husband's portraits. Otherwise there is virtually no record of her, because her successor, Alice Hoschedé, who kept watch with Monet over her body (and was described by the Monet expert Daniel Wildenstein as a 'possessive and jealous woman'), made the painter destroy Camille's entire correspondence, in order to reign 'unchallenged over Monet's life'.[53] Even with this statement in mind, reading Alice's letters makes one wonder why, in view of her many and varied demands, commands, little jealousies and claims to possessions, Monet now settled down with this woman and what his motives were for marrying her some years later. Was it for comfort and the need for someone to look after him and his two children? It would have been cheaper and less problematic to engage a housekeeper. Did Monet, who outwardly appeared self-confident and high-spirited, need a partner to dominate him and tell him what to do, rather like Richard Strauss? His letters in reply to Alice's frequent tall orders and unreasonable demands are often conciliatory, meek and apologetically flattering, which seems to indicate that this was so. Over and over again in the following years Monet gave in to Alice's often petty wishes and demands – for the sake of a quiet life? Did he need this woman as a dominatrix? How much did she understand about his art? Did she praise or constructively criticise the new pictures he showed her? We know no more about her attitude to his painting than we do about Camille's.

After Camille's death Alice Hoschedé had a free hand over Monet's life and used the opportunity to make herself indispensable by looking after his two sons and running the household in Vétheuil. Ostensibly she was still a married woman, whose luckless husband spent most of his time in Paris and only now and then appeared on the scene in Vétheuil, perhaps mainly to prevent possible gossip by giving the outward appearance of married life. Through the years of the family's ambivalent situation Hoschedé apparently still entertained the hope and illusion that his wife would return to him. One can only guess how far the couple's estrangement was due to his financial failure. After her husband's bankruptcy did Alice, who came from a well-off family, turn more and more to Monet, to whom the future belonged, for the care of her own children as well?

The first winter after Camille's death was unusually severe. The Seine froze over and the thaw in January 1880 caused enormous blocks of ice to form near Vétheuil. In spite of the cold Monet went out every day to paint. A whole series of pictures bear witness to this strange natural phenomenon. As in the previous year, Vétheuil and its environs served Monet in the warmer season as an inspiration for landscape paintings. Not until 1881 did he again go to the Normandy coast to paint.

Gradually his financial situation improved. The 1880 Salon accepted one of his pictures and in June the magazine 'La Vie Moderne' hung 18 of his works in its offices. Georges Charpentier, the owner, was a patron of Renoir's. Madame Charpentier bought the picture by Monet exhibited in the Salon as a present for her husband. In August the Le Havre art gallery displayed three of his works. Yet although his income in 1881 came to over 20,000 francs, he now had to feed at least ten mouths and still could not make ends meet. When in the spring of 1881 he found he was not in a position to pay the next instalment of rent in Vétheuil, he decided to move house and did so at the end of the year after his summer trips to Normandy.

After consulting Zola, who was knowledgeable about such places, Monet chose Poissy, about 20 kilometres northwest of Paris – a place which offered him little artistic inspiration and apparently mainly served as a temporary, and above all cheap, refuge. But this move had another significance: Alice, who in

Vétheuil could maintain the outward appearance of still being married, moved to Poissy with him against her husband's wishes. It was now clear to Hoschedé that she had made her choice in favour of Monet.

After shunning the sixth Impressionist exhibition the previous year, Monet contributed 30 works to the seventh in the spring of 1882. The critics praised him highly, though still with reservations. The pictures from Vétheuil and the most recent seascapes were particularly successful. Again in 1882 he worked on the Normandy coast – first in Dieppe and Pourville, and again in the latter resort with his extended family for several months during the summer. In the neighbouring town of Varengeville he painted a number of brightly coloured pictures which heralded a new, more spontaneous style. He had now overcome his recent artistic crisis as well.

In 1882 Monet earned about 25,000, but the increase in income still did not cover his large outgoings. Durand-Ruel was in temporary difficulties with payment, due to a banking scandal, and at the beginning of the year had been compelled to stop making purchases. Monet therefore had to turn to his private collectors, but by the summer payments had begun to come in again from the art-dealer, who in March of the following year mounted a solo exhibition for Monet at his Paris gallery. When Édouard Manet died in Paris on 30 April, Monet was moving house and hurried to the capital for the funeral of his older colleague, with whom (after some initial reserve on Manet's part) he had lately enjoyed an increasingly close personal and artistic relationship. After Bazille's early death Manet had repeatedly helped the younger man with money, arranged sales for him or bought pictures from him for himself. He also visited him now and again, especially in Argenteuil where he learnt much from Monet's plein-air painting and Impressionism. Monet, Zola, the painter Henri Fantin-Latour and the critic Théodore

Duret together carried Manet's coffin to its grave.

On his frequent rail journeys to the Normandy coast Monet had passed through the little town of Vernon on the Seine and since Poissy had nothing more to hold him, he was looking seriously in that area for the right place to paint and to live. In April 1883 he found it, in the form of the little village of Giverny with its 290 inhabitants, not far from where a stream called the Epte flowed into the Seine, about 80 kilometres northwest of Paris and halfway from there to Rouen. His earlier homes in Argenteuil, Vétheuil and Poissy lay much nearer to Paris.

The varied and pleasant countryside around Giverny must have convinced Monet that plenty of themes awaited him there. A country-house with a large orchard on the road from Vernon to Gisors so captivated him on his first visit that he called on the owner, Louis-Joseph Singeot and rented it. It was a long building painted pink, with eight rooms on its two main floors, two attics, a cellar and a storehouse. On the east side were two sheds and washrooms and on the west a barn which he turned into a studio. The property also included a smaller farm building with several rooms. There was therefore enough space for all the members of the double family. The children were sent to either day or boarding schools in Vernon or Giverny. For his boats and travelling painting equipment Monet had a barn built about a kilometre away on the Seine, to enable him to paint by the water.

He furnished the house sparsely but with good taste, decorating the yellow-painted dining-room with his coloured Japanese woodcuts, which still hang in the same places. On this property, which he bought in 1890 at the age of 42, set among the gardens which he stocked, laid out and enlarged with ever-increasing lavishness and careful planning over the next decades, Monet spent the second half of his life, apart from his travels in search of new subjects to paint, which became rarer as the years went by.

Here also he died and was buried. It was firstly the surroundings of Giverny which provided the principal subjects for his painting, but later more and more exclusively his garden.

MAJOR PAINTING JOURNEYS

At the end of 1883 a new world of painting opened up for Monet, when in December he and Renoir went on a short trip to the Mediterranean. They visited their mutual friend Cézanne in L'Estaque and travelled as far as Genoa. Monet was particularly taken with Bordighera on the Riviera, with its enchanting situation and tropical vegetation. Although during this first, short stay he painted several pictures, he commented briefly on it in a letter to Durand-Ruel on 12 January 1884 in the following terms: *The pleasanter it has been to travel as a tourist with Renoir, the more irritating it would be to do so in order to work together. I have always worked better in solitude and following my own impressions.*[54]

A day later he was off again to Bordighera, where he stayed in an English boarding-house. In the little town he was particularly charmed by a large and lavish flower garden belonging to a Signor Moreno, who gave him permission to paint there and was very hospitable, inviting him to meals and driving him about. Happy and inspired, Monet threw himself into his work. His sensitive painter's eyes, accustomed to the often misty and sombre north, first had to acclimatise themselves and his letters home tell of the effort this required: *The palm-trees are driving me crazy; the motifs are extremely difficult to capture. {...} As to the blue of the sea and the sky, it's impossible. {...} I am working very, very hard, because I haven't yet grasped the colours of this country; I sometimes feel terrified by the paints that I am compelled to use.*[55] By the beginning of February he already felt that he was making progress and that not just new scenery but also a whole new artistic realm was opening up for him: *. . . I think my first studies are very bad; they are laboriously created but they have also taught me how*

Claude Monet 1883

to look. { . . . } I am in a fairyland here, and I have absolutely no idea
where to look first. Everything is extraordinarily beautiful and I would like
to paint it all. I am using and wasting a lot of paint. One has to try things
out. The landscape here is something completely new to me, to be studied, and
I am just beginning to find my feet and it is terribly difficult to know where
I am going and what I can do; you need diamonds and jewels on your
palette. As for blue and pink, here they are.[56]

    After three months Monet returned to Giverny with a rich harvest of

about 50 paintings. Just before leaving he had discovered Cap Martin,
which he thought delightful and 'discovering' which he kept for a later
return to the Mediterranean.

Having found his new permanent home, the seasonal pattern
of Monet's family life and his creative work became increasingly
tranquil. Any year-by-year description of the second half of his life
would be monotonous. In the 1880s through into part of the
1890s the normal rhythm in Giverny was only interrupted by
painting trips, which became more and more infrequent towards
the turn of the century, due to Monet's changing artistic vision as
well as the problems of age. He had a robust constitution but his
decades of working in the open air in wind and weather at all
times of year had naturally taken its toll of his health, resulting in
rheumatic complaints in his later years. Serial painting in the
immediate vicinity of his house, which became more and more
characteristic of this period in his life, to a great extent resulted
from the limitations set by his physical condition.

However at first he was still exhausting himself with journeys
which sapped his strength: in the autumn of 1884 to Etretat, the
following spring a third, though shorter, trip to Holland, in
November 1887 two weeks in London. It was not until January
1888 that he fulfilled his desire to revisit the Mediterranean coast.
On the Côte d'Azur, particularly at Antibes and Cap Martin, he
painted a second group of southern landscapes of even more
impressive quality. By a curious coincidence Vincent van Gogh
had settled in the neighbourhood at the same time to begin on his
incomparable mature works, also inspired by the southern sun,
vegetation and colours. Through his Parisian art-dealer brother
Théo he knew that Monet was staying nearby.

At the beginning of 1888 Théo van Gogh had signed a contract
with Monet to mount his first solo exhibition in his branch of
Goupil's (Boussod & Valadon) in the Boulevard Montmartre in
Paris in the second half of June. Monet had sold him 10 of the 40

pictures he had painted in and around Antibes for about 1200 francs each. A clause in the contract gave the painter 50 per cent of the profit if Goupil sold any of them – a new departure for Monet, accustomed as he was to contracts which were to his financial disadvantage. But the fact that ever since his first Paris exhibition in Georges Petit's gallery in 1885 he had allowed other dealers besides Durand-Ruel to handle his works demonstrates the painter's greater self-confidence, now that he was in demand. Understandably, Durand-Ruel was not pleased by his most important living artist 'playing away' but the fact that he put up with the situation betrays a measure of tolerance which is not frequently to be found in art-dealers. However there was plenty coming Durand-Ruel's way, in spite of these 'excursions' of Monet's. On the occasion of important exhibitions in the following years, Durand-Ruel found himself repeatedly collaborating with his Parisian and foreign competitors. Business shared is always better than no business at all.

Through Théo van Gogh's initiative a Monet exhibition comprising 20 of his pictures was held at the London branch of Goupil's in February 1889, and in the autumn of that year Théo sold one of Monet's paintings for the astonishing sum of 10,000 francs – the highest amount paid to date for one of the painter's works. Théo's early death in January 1891 put an end to this wave of success with Goupil's.

'When he [Théo] wrote to his brother that the naturalist writer Guy de Maupassant, whom Vincent greatly admired, had come to see the exhibition, Vincent replied that, for him, Maupassant was to Zola what Vermeer was to Rembrandt.'[57] Monet had also met Maupassant by chance in Etretat in October 1885. The writer and the painter had the shared experience of childhoods spent in Normandy and they show an affinity in their themes as well as in their description of atmosphere. We keep finding in Maupassant's novels and short stories descriptions of scenes which we know through Monet's pictures–for instance, the rowing regatta at Argenteuil. In his article *The Life of a Landscape Painter*, published in 1886, Maupassant described the way Monet worked, which he had observed in Etretat.[58] Van Gogh in his letters often commented on the similarity between Monet's painting and Maupassant's way with words.[59]

In the 1880s there was in fact an interchange between Monet and a number of Parisian literary figures. On 17 November 1884 he met the writer Octave Mirbeau, an admirer of his works who in the following years frequently wrote flattering articles about him. During a long and fruitful period painting on Belle-Ile off the coast of Brittany in 1886 Monet met the Parisian critic Gustave Geffroy, already an admirer of his work who, after knowing Monet for decades in Giverny, in 1922 published the first biography of the painter.[60]

It was also in 1886 that Monet first met the symbolist poet Stéphane Mallarmé, who wrote appreciatively to the painter after visiting the Goupil exhibition in the summer of 1888: 'I left enchanted with the work you did last winter; I have rated what you do above everything else for a long time, but I believe you are now in your best period ever. Oh! Yes, as poor Édouard [Manet] liked to reiterate: Monet has genius.'[61] Mallarmé owned some of Monet's works. In a 1900 photograph of the poet in his apartment there is on the wall beside him a landscape by the painter he so admired, who in 1890 had given it to him as a present. Mallarmé once sent Monet a letter with the following verse on the envelope in place of the recipient's correct address:

> *Monsieur Monet, whose vision is deceived*
> *by neither winter nor summer,*
> *Lives and paints in Giverny,*
> *Near Vernon, in the Eure.*[62]

Even in old age Monet was amazed and impressed that the letter actually reached him.

Émile Zola, who had followed Monet's career since the 1860s

Stéphane Mallarmé in his Paris apartment. A Monet landscape
hangs on the left hand wall

with extremely positive reviews of his exhibitions, published in
1886 his novel *L'Œuvre*, in which the protagonist was a failed
painter, clearly an Impressionist modelled mainly on Cézanne,
whom he had known since childhood, but also on Manet. The
painters whom Zola had for years been supporting through his
writings felt betrayed and insulted by the maliciously overdrawn
character in the novel. Cézanne thanked Zola briefly for sending
him the book and broke off their friendship without another
word. Manet had died three years before and could therefore not
defend himself and Monet was the only Impressionist who wrote
to Zola to protest. Zola, by now well established and haughty,
(though even his admirer van Gogh strongly questioned his
artistic judgement)[63], played virtually no further part in promoting
Impressionism or commenting on it in his writings. Unlike other

fellow artists – for example the anti-semitic Degas – Monet remained a political ally of Zola's, as became clear during the Dreyfus Affair a decade later.

When Monet learnt in 1889 that Manet's impoverished widow was about to sell *Olympia* – the painting which once caused such a scandal –for 20,000 francs to America, he exerted himself to keep the work in France, and indeed in Paris. He was unhappy and even bitter to see his own paintings being offered by Durand-Ruel to the USA and sold for high prices there, because they were *leaving for the land of the Yankees.*[64] He organised a subscription for the Manet work, which quickly raised the 20,000 francs necessary to rescue it, and offered it to the Louvre. After some petty and unworthy wrangling, it was finally agreed that the picture should be put on display at the Musée du Luxembourg, because an artist had to have been dead for ten years before his works could be allowed through the hallowed portals of the Louvre.

After his spring painting expedition to Antibes – the most important and rewarding to date – Monet visited the writer Maurice Rollinat in Fresselines, where the valley of the River Creuse strongly inspired him to paint. Here he produced a series of pictures, mostly of the same subject, which were his first depicting the same motif at different times of day and in different kinds of weather. This was the beginning of the second period of Monet's creative output – though he had not planned it as such – which consisted almost exclusively in series of paintings of the same subject. That very year Monet began to create one such series, of a row of poplars on the banks of the Epte near Giverny, in varying colours and atmospheres. In the 1890s there followed a series of pictures of haystacks; in 1892 the views of Rouen Cathedral and from 1896 a series painted by a tributary of the Seine near Giverny, entitled *Morning on the Seine* or *Arm of the Seine near Giverny*. In the next year he painted the first pictures of water lilies on his pond at Giverny. This was to be his principal subject in the last 30 years of his life, together with other aspects of the garden, which with ever-increasing commitment he enlarged and transformed into a flowering paradise.

Having not painted on the Normandy coast for a number of years, at the age of 55 Monet embarked on a nostalgic journey to his former subjects at Varengeville, Pourville and Dieppe and again in January of the following year stayed in Pourville. In 1900 and 1901 in Vétheuil he returned to the themes which he had found there almost two decades before – this time in serial form. London, where he had first stayed in 1870/1 and done only minor work, must have now attracted him again, for in the autumn of 1899 he began painting views of the Thames from the window of his room in the Savoy Hotel and continued doing so until 1901. His last great painting expedition took him in 1908 to Venice, whence he returned with pictures which he subsequently completed at home, as he did his London paintings.

THE LAST YEARS

After his great painting tours of the 1880s, Monet's second and last period – strictly speaking, it began when he settled at Giverny in 1883 – was less restless and eventful from 1890 on than the earlier period of struggle as an Impressionist had been. Now that he was comfortably off he could concentrate more on painting undisturbed and developing his property. The rhythm of the years was now marked by successful solo exhibitions and participation in general exhibitions at home and abroad, which the influential critics reviewed in almost unanimously positive and even enthusiastic terms. He was selling more pictures for higher prices and being publicly honoured. The first museum to acquire one of his paintings was the Oslo Nasjonalgalleriet, which in 1890 bought a landscape, *Etretat in the Rain* (1886).

A regular stream of visitors came to Giverny, including his

Monet in front of his house in the Gardens at Giverny: 1923

principal art-dealer Durand-Ruel, who bought his pictures and discussed ideas for exhibitions with him, and old and new buyers and collectors, among them celebrities and wealthy foreign art-lovers, from Japan to the USA. Critics and journalists also came through his door, interviewing him and writing up his comments at such length that one wonders, in this age of tape-recorders, how literally they reported his words in their publications. In several of these interviews there are contradictions and discrepancies which may well be due to lack of accuracy on the part of the interviewer rather than to gaps in Monet's own memory. Yet these testimonies are important and also informative about the self-knowledge of the 'Prince of Painters', who at the age of 60, now that he was recognised and revered as a painter, deliberately (very differently from his youthful descriptions) wanted to portray himself in a particular light and even looked back with some bitterness. *Yes, my friend, today I cannot paint enough, and probably make £15,000 a year; 20 years ago I was starving.*[65]

After the turn of the century French painters of the next generation were among the admiring visitors to Giverny – for instance, Henri Matisse, Albert Marquet, Ker Xavier Roussel, Pierre Bonnard and Édouard Vuillard. They all swam in Monet's stylistic slipstream for a while (Bonnard permanently) and paid tribute to their idol. Monet, for his part, warmed to some of his emulators, above all Vuillard and Marquet, and even bought paintings from them. He also bought more paintings from his own contemporaries and fellow-campaigners, above all from Cézanne, whose significance he had recognised early on. Together with him and with van Gogh, Monet stands today on the highest level of all in any hierarchy of art history. In the end he owned a dozen Cézannes and, among others, four Manets, nine Renoirs, three Pissarros and works by Daubigny, Corot, Delacroix, Boudin, Jongkind, Degas, Sisley and Paul Signac. It is worth noting that Monet the landscape painter mainly bought figurative paintings from his colleagues.

Monet spent his increasing wealth not only on good food, which he had always greatly enjoyed, but also on travelling in luxury and in 1900 started buying motor-cars, in which he went for drives on Sundays and also undertook longer journeys. He did not drive himself, but engaged chauffeurs to do so.

After the highly acclaimed appearance of the first serial pictures in the early 1890s, many of Monet's former colleagues and admirers expressed reservations, not appreciating his repetitions of the same subject for what they were: a novel artistic concept and a venture into new territory. Above all people were afraid that success might make Monet too comfortable and idle, as he was almost entirely repeating and creating variations on the same, easily saleable pictures. Although one should not underestimate this danger, a retrospective look through Monet's complete œuvre will disclose that the individual serial paintings are not just repetitions, but constituent parts of an overarching artistic concept. He himself, having had to sell off many of his pictures cheaply and often before they were finished in his years of privation, had now become increasingly self-critical and destroyed a significant number of pictures which he did not want to work on any more or which he felt he could not even salvage by over-painting them. This often horrified the art-dealers who had already reckoned on exhibiting or selling those works.

In March 1891 Ernest Hoschedé, by then a cripple, died in Paris in curious circumstances, for Alice, still officially his wife, was with him in his last hours and he died at 45 Rue Laffite, the

Monet and his wife Alice, St Mark's Square, Venice:1908

birthplace of his rival Monet. Alice had her husband buried at Giverny. On 16 June 1892 she and Monet were married in a civil ceremony there, so legalising their life together which they had actually been leading for more than a decade. The Monets travelled together to London in 1899, to Spain in 1904 and to Venice in 1908, but in 1909 Alice contracted leukaemia and died on 19 May 1911 at Giverny. This plunged Monet, who in spite of his strong will was obviously psychologically very depen-

dant on Alice, into a lengthy crisis, during which he painted very little and even considered giving up his art altogether, as he wrote to his stepdaughter Blanche Hoschedé on 4 December 1911: *Painting completely disgusts me and I am going to throw away my brushes and paints for ever. Everything I have been able to do recently was to spoil some pictures of Venice completely, so that I had to destroy them; a sad event. I should have left them as they were, in memory of the happy days I spent there with my dear Alice . . . I am suffering so much and I well know how terribly naive my wretched painting is. I cannot say that otherwise everything is going well, because nothing is going well, as I cannot sleep and the days are as long as the evenings and nights.*[66]

He was now over 70 and could look back on a great body of work. However, soon after fate dealt him a second blow when his elder son Jean, who was married to Blanche Hoschedé, died at Giverny in 1914 from venereal disease. Monet was closely involved in Jean's death, for both he and Michel, like many children of famous fathers, were condemned to exist in the shadow of their domineering parent. The success of both their lives was more or less superficial, like others whose calling was to be someone's son.

When the First World War broke out in August 1914, Monet's stepson Jean-Pierre Hoschedé was called up and soon after Michel Monet volunteered for military service. A 1916 photograph shows the 75 year-old Monet with the two soldiers on a bench at Giverny. In the photograph is also Blanche Hoschedé, who after Jean's death devoted herself entirely to looking after her stepfather and father-in-law.

In the pre-war years there were signs that Monet's eyesight was deteriorating – the most terrible affliction for a painter. His fellow-campaigner Degas had been virtually blind since 1906 and unable to paint; all he could do was make sculptures by feel. Pissarro, who died in 1903, had also had problems with his eyes in his last years. Encouraged by his friend Georges Clemenceau, Prime Minister of France since 1917, he went on painting, undeterred by his failing eyesight and even, in the middle of the war when materials were scarce, buying an additional plot of land on which to build himself a third, spacious studio to hold the large-scale painting of water lilies he was planning. Here he created an overwhelmingly large series of decorative paintings in the years remaining to him.

Monet had already met Georges Clemenceau when the latter

Clemenceau, Monet and Lily Butler on the Japanese Bridge
in the Gardens at Giverny: 1921

was a journalist, in whose paper *La Justice* Gustave Geffroy, among others, had published articles about him. In Monet's later years this developed into one of his very few acquaintanceship with anyone who was not a fellow-painter. Monet, always self-assured and not socially at ease, was basically a loner. Apart from his wives Camille and Alice and the children who came into his life through them, he kept his distance from his fellow human beings. With Bazille, his closest friend to whom he owed so much, he used the formal mode of address until Bazille's early death. Distance separated him from Renoir in the second half of his life and only in 1908 did the two old comrades see each other again, when Monet visited him in Cagnes on the Mediterranean when returning from Venice.

Now, during Monet's last decade, it was the art-loving Clemenceau who frequently kept the afflicted painter company at Giverny. Countless photographs show the two old men pacing round the garden together. It must have been an unexpected honour for Monet to be friends with the Prime Minister and to be flattered and admired by him. Official state honours had never impressed Monet: in 1888 he had refused the proffered membership of the Legion of Honour, repeating this refusal when the offer was later renewed. In 1920 he also declined a seat in the French Institute.

When Clemenceau failed in his candidature for the presidency of France in 1920, as a retired politician he had more time to pay visits to Giverny. He persuaded Monet to donate the majority of his monumental water lily murals to the state. After lengthy wrangling over where in Paris to install the cycle, the contract was eventually finalised. However, Monet retained the works for the rest of his life – perhaps because he was superstitious or afraid of death – and continued working on individual pictures almost to the end.

In 1912 cataract in both eyes was diagnosed, making an early operation desirable, but Monet kept postponing it because he feared that it might result in his completely losing his sight but eventually it was at least partly restored through two operations, in

January and July of 1923. His eye surgeon, Doctor Charles Coutela, then experimented with a variety of tinted lenses made by Zeiss (therefore from the Germany which Monet had so hated since the two wars), which allowed him to distinguish passably well between colours and virtually to complete the decorative canvases.

In 1926 Monet fell ill with an incurable lung disease and his

Monet in his third studio in front of the great 'Water Lilies' decoration. 1921

strength quickly failed. On 5 December 1926 at the age of 86 he died in the arms of his friend Clemenceau, who happened to be present. A few days later he was buried in the Giverny graveyard beside Hoschedé and Alice, without any ceremony, as he had wished. The water lily paintings were taken to Paris shortly afterwards and in a dedication ceremony on 17 May 1927 were installed in the Orangery as Monet's bequest to the State.

The Single Pictures: A Renewal of Painting

In all Claude Monet left about 2000 oil paintings. Beside this astonishing output of a long artistic life other genres play a minor part. As his youthful works show, Monet could certainly have become an outstanding draughtsman, but lines soon faded into the background as he increasingly emphasised the fleeting element and the merging of colour formations into each other. His later occasional monochrome chalk drawings and coloured pastels were casual sidelines. A series of notebooks contain swift, sketchy outlines, mostly in pencil and mainly studies for paintings. Monet seems not to have been interested in graphic printing.

It is curious and puzzling that the Impressionists, and in particular Monet, hardly ever painted in water-colours, although that simple technique lends itself to conveying spontaneity and would therefore have suited their striving after swift realisation of momentary moods better than the technically more difficult and slower technique of oil painting.

CARICATURES

Claude Monet's artistic work began with his schoolboy drawings, most importantly his caricatures. He started in 1856 and the first date to be found on any of them is 1857. He must have completed well over a hundred. Those which survive are mostly of prominent Parisians – politicians, artists or eccentrics – who featured in the newspapers. Monet followed a variety of examples, such as the 'Panthéon', a series of caricatures by the photographer and artist

Nadar, or works by Hadol or Carjat. The budding artist does not seem, however, to have studied the caricatures of the great Honoré Daumier, but in fact he did adopt a current style of caricaturing which Daumier himself had used in his early works: a large head with exaggerated features resting on a disproportionately smaller body, foreshortened by perspective. The subject is represented as a marionette or homunculus with a monstrous head.

Although in many ways Monet's work is influenced by his forerunners, his caricatures are highly accomplished in draughtsmanship and original in form. Most are drawn with a soft pencil, using subtle, 'artistic' shading; plasticity and depth of focus are emphasised with white highlights and exotic or curious elements with coloured washes. Many of the subjects stand in front of light, undefined backgrounds on which their shadows fall and where in some cases there are objects to explain something about them.

These originals were not for sale but intended by Monet for his own study. The bulk of the surviving sheets come from his own archive, while only a smaller number of the commissioned works he sold have survived, perhaps because later collectors were misled by the signature 'O Monet'.

PORTRAITS

It is both astonishing and noteworthy that Monet, who was later principally famous for his landscapes, began his career with, among other things, figurative painting, especially portraits. After his youthful caricatures, portraits form the main body of his work in the 1860s – the decade of searching and embarking on the road to Impressionism – together with still lifes and landscapes. These portraits are no caricatures, but careful and faithful likenesses of the sitter.

Six conventional portraits survive, painted between 1862 and 1865, but Monet's *Portrait of Victor Jacquemont Holding a Parasol* of 1865 demonstrates that he was capable of something more. It is a full-length likeness, over a metre high, of a young man in elegant street clothes with straw hat and parasol, a black-and-white pointer beside him, walking on a path through a park or wood, where bright sunlight falls through the leaves of the trees. The smooth style in which the figure is painted and the exquisite colour-scheme – bottle-green trousers, tan jacket and waistcoat, yellow cravat and straw hat – together with details such as the ring on his finger, the flower in his buttonhole and his moustache, make a dandified effect. The picture exudes youthful, carefree summertime. It is one of Monet's early masterpieces.

After at least seven more portraits in the late 1860s and 1870s – probably mostly done as commissions or favours – in 1880 Monet painted two half-length portraits of the factory-owner Coqueret and his son, the tranquil mood of which betrays the example of Renoir as clearly as do the portraits of Paul and Eugénie Graff which he painted in Pourville in 1882. The subjects were the proprietor and chef of the simple hotel where Monet was staying and his wife, whom he painted with her white dog. These half-length portraits facing each other are both sketches made in light colours, indicating that they are a pair. At the time Monet was only rarely painting portraits and he called the picture of the cook a *curious sketch.*[67] Having painted a some-what more conventional portrait of an English painter with a full beard in Bordighera in 1884, he went on to make an evocative picture of Poly, the 57-year old factotum who carried all his painting equipment for him. The subject, in half-length and obviously seated against a light, delicately coloured and structured background, is wearing a blue pullover and dark hat, and has a dishevelled beard, red nose and red cheeks. He looks comically sceptical, as though he did not think much of what the painter sitting opposite him was doing. But this is a masterly portrait and makes one regret that Monet has left us so few paintings of people.

Although until then his portraits had been either commissions or – rarely – casual pieces of work, Monet did paint a number of portraits of his family on his own account. The first of these was the 1866 life-size full-length portrait *Camille or the Woman with a Green Dress*. It is highly realistic but wholly untypical of Monet's portraits before and since in the precision with which he painted the material of her dress, the mysterious chiaroscuro and the somewhat sentimental bearing of the subject, who seems to be gliding past the painter in a melancholy, pensive mood. This is a virtuoso painting done for effect, designed to open the doors of the Salon and thus to give Monet the breakthrough he needed. In this respect he was only moderately successful, because in the long run it was not the conventional, bourgeois route that led to his fame.[68]

However, this portrait did bring him some material advantage, because two years after it was exhibited he received a commission to paint the wife of the Le Havre businessman and art-collector Louis-Joachim Gaudibert. There is no doubt that this work was modelled on Camille's portrait and indeed the commission may even have stipulated that he should produce something similar to the Salon picture. In fact the composition, style and spirit of these two portraits – both over two metres high – are all too similar:

'Madame Louis Joachim Gaudibert,' 1868. Musée d'Orsay, Paris

like Camille, Madame Gaudibert appears in dreamy profile, in a somewhat affected pose. The light-brown material (silk?) of her dress is painstakingly detailed and over it she wears a red-patterned shawl. In contrast to the dark portrait of Camille, the scene is set in cool, light tones. The pale blue of the curtains, reflected in the flower-patterned carpet, convey nothing of the mysteriousness of Camille's portrait. Not only is this later portrait overloaded with accessories, its subject is so obviously posing artificially that the general effect is pretentious and embarrassing – a rich man having his wife painted in a manner appropriate to her standing. The larger portrait of Camille, however conventional, is infinitely more accomplished and more intimate.

Monet painted some other portraits of Camille: first in 1866 – possibly as a study for the great Salon picture – came a half-length picture in profile, showing his mistress against a dark background with her little white dog in her arms – a work which Monet kept all his life and which is much more expressive and vivid than the large, posed portrait. In 1875 he painted another two-metre high, life-size, full-length portrait of her in Japanese costume with a blond wig and open fan, in a somewhat theatrically affected pose in front of an indoor wall decorated with fans (Boston). This picture, which seizes on and indeed exploits the current enthusiasm and fashion for all things Japanese, is certainly Monet's most subservient work, bordering on kitsch. The choice of bright colours, the artificial pose, the exotic, theatrical setting and the decorative character of the whole represent the peak of spurious sham and pandering to the public. It is an isolated piece within Monet's œuvre.

Monet's last portrait of his ailing wife in 1877 is another Renoiresque three-quarter length picture of her seated in a room. This is an Impressionist work in reds and blues, much less pretentious than the two large earlier portraits. The spontaneously painted study of the dead Camille is heart-rending. This is no portrait in the real sense of the word: it is a ghostly portrayal of the mortal remains of a beloved person who seems to be dissolving in light and shade.

Monet apparently painted no portraits of his second wife, Alice Hoschedé. Does this indicate a completely different relationship between these two? Being jealous and domineering, like Egon Schiele's wife and the wives of some other painters, Alice forbade her husband to engage professional models, probably with the fatal result of his giving up portraiture and figure painting. Of the children in his household – his two and Alice's four – he made a mere dozen little likenesses reminiscent of Renoir. In 1874 he painted his brother Léon as a bourgeois businessman with bowler hat and stiff collar. The bearded face in quarter profile in this half-length painting resembles many of the photographs of the mature Claude Monet himself.

Monet painted very few self-portraits. Apart from one unfinished picture of a sitting figure, which Wildenstein dogmatically attributes to Monet but which does not fit with his style of portraiture at all and may have been done by his English colleague John Singer Sargent, only two self-portraits survive: one from 1886 when he was 45 in a dark beret and grey artist's smock, the other a sketchy image with a white beard against an unfinished background, which was the only one in a minor series of portraits of himself in old age to escape his mania for destruction. What a contrast between the two! In the first is a man in the prime of life, with a vigorous and challenging look, painted in delicate shades of light brown and grey-blue and in the other, painted in 1917, an old man, a study in stronger colours, the paint applied vigorously and thickly.

STILL LIFE

As with portraiture, it was mainly in his early and middle years that Monet devoted himself to this other traditional genre. The artistic creativity of the man who was later to become principally a landscape painter actually began with still lifes – ideal for beginners to practise composition, painting technique and the use of colour. Instead of being spontaneously dashed off like his youthful caricatures, here Monet the beginner had to find the patience to develop the required classical painting technique of glazing. This he did through still life compositions arranged in his studio. Interestingly, he painted crockery and any kind of food. For the six surviving still lifes from 1861/2 this future gourmet mainly chose meat products – a cutlet, a piece of raw meat, kidneys, eggs and butter – and dead game birds in three still lifes of hunting subjects.

In the most representative and largest work in this genre (Paris), his dog is sniffing at pheasants, partridges and blackcock laid out on a marble console under hunting equipment hanging on the wall. The dog's head acts as a magnet to draw the viewer's eye into the picture. This study undoubtedly reflects the still lifes of the 17th- and 18th-century masters which Monet would have seen in the Louvre when he was 21. In his early attempts at the genre he also employed and elaborated on the compositional principles of the old masters as well: dividing the canvas by arranging his subjects vertically, horizontally and diagonally, while blending them into a harmonious whole. In these studies Monet systematically developed and executed the painstaking technique and traditional principles of composition combined with using light to suggest spatial dimension. In these works the young man wanted to prove that there was something to him, that he had talent, not only to his sceptical father but also to the established artists who awaited him in Paris as patrons and teachers. These early still lifes were the entry tickets to his artistic career.

Monet only occasionally included still lifes in his work in the following decades, mostly as isolated individual pieces or in small groups. In 1866, however, came a completely unusual work in the context of his overall output: the still life with a jar of peaches painted, like the studies he did as a beginner, in the glazed style of the old masters, is striking in its dualism of trompe-œil in the middle distance – one can almost feel the peaches' velvety texture – and the bold *alla prima* painting of the foreground details (white marbling on the surface of a dark table). The colours are now, five years after the first studies, extremely delicate: a juxtaposition of warm tones (the fruit) and cooler, blue-green shades (the surroundings). Even more strongly than in the large, early still life with game, he here stresses an almost geometric severity of composition, with two vertical lines meeting the main horizontal line, which is 'echoed' more faintly in the upper edge of the preserving jar. This arrangement is more in the style of Cézanne than any of Monet's other works.

Monet later made some more hunting and fruit still lifes and combinations of the two (for example a work from 1867), followed by two of fruit only. All these three were like Cézanne's compositions: on the surface of a table covered in a white cloth, which runs horizontally across the lower half of the picture, baskets and fruit have been arranged, the textures comparatively realistically reproduced but already slightly blending artistically into each other.

The same applies to two still lifes from 1869 of two fishes on a white cloth and a dead pheasant draped on a white-covered table. This was the year of Monet's radical shift into Impressionism, which is even more striking in a still life with fruit and a garland of flowers, painted in the same year. While the relatively compactly painted vessels (fruit basket and flower vase) and the dark background represent the old, realist principle, the fruit and the flowers are already freer in their colours and painting technique, which he develops further towards dissolution of form, greater brightness and intensified colours in six later fruit still lifes from 1872, 1879 and 1880. These are Impressionist paintings in the truest sense. That there are so few of them was not only due to Monet's preference for landscape painting, but doubtless also because solid 'dead' objects are more difficult to reproduce in an atmosphere of 'momentariness' than free, living nature. That Monet, when he did occasionally choose this genre, in most cases did not select man-made objects but products of nature in the widest sense – animals, fruit and flowers – is definitely not a coincidence, for they also appear in their natural environment in his landscapes.

Meanwhile Monet the gourmet was repeatedly painting hunting still lifes – like Courbet, whom he admired. For instance, in 1870 he arranged a wild boar's head with a sword-shaped dagger in a martial manner. Two years later came a still life with birds reminiscent of the trompe-œil works of Jacopo de' Barbari; a hanging partridge and snipe cast their shadows on the white wall, but in contrast to their historical predecessors are not painstakingly reproduced in trompe-œil manner, but with artistic licence in delicately merging shades of red, mauve and blue. In three very similarly composed hunting still lifes from 1879 Monet arranged several recently shot or purchased pheasants, but without matching the charm of the composition and artistry of the partridge still life of 1872. The three pictures seem more like dutiful studies: the birds had to be painted before they were prepared and eaten.

Monet's last, major works in this genre were the many panels he had to paint between 1882 and 1885 for the drawing-room doors of Durand-Ruel's house. Most of this decorative series consisted of flowers but Monet included some still life subjects as well, mostly returning to themes he had used previously, such as two pheasants hanging on the wall, or fruit in baskets, on plates, grouped together or on their branches. Here in a planned, commissioned decorative work there occurred what a few years later was to happen in Monet's œuvre in general: moving from single pictures to decorative series in which the components are subordinated to the whole and thus greatly restricted and reduced in their individual expression. The realistic branch with fruit – however delicately portrayed in form and colour – has been downgraded into an ornamental garland.

Two almost identical still lifes with eggs from 1907 are final latecomers to this genre and follow the serial principle which Monet had meanwhile completely absorbed and developed – the same subject presented in differently coloured light. As also with the series of landscapes predominant in his work at that time, the subject is only an excuse for creating variations in colour and form; these are abstract, still life landscapes.

FLOWERS

In the same way Monet quite compulsively developed flower painting as a special form of still life and these works started to appear when he was first a student. Flowers were favourite subjects, closely observed and copied. Together with his friend Renoir he painted flowers meticulously in the 1860s, and one large-scale representative piece has survived – a veritable cornucopia of spring flowers against a dark background, a cascade of precisely reproduced blooms in realist style. The carpet-like composition anticipates the large serial paintings of chrysanthemums in that it is a decorative sequence of patches of colour strewn over the canvas. The abstract painter Ernst Wilhelm Nay was later to express himself in a similar, though smaller way.

'Chrysanthemum
Bed,' 1897.
Kunstmuseum,
Basel

After his early studies in this genre, Monet took up flower painting again relatively late in life and in 1878 produced four pieces, of which three are of relatively small flowers in open vases, while in two long pictures the actual blooms compete with the flower-patterned carpet in the background. The fourth flower painting, of 1878, is however a vertical composition, which Monet elaborated on several times in the following years: out of a slender vase in the foreground decorative flowers emerge, sprout and grow upwards. Having varied this thematic idea in 1879 in two pictures of nasturtiums, he turned it in 1880 into seven masterly flower paintings, which are his most important in this genre and also his Impressionist flower pictures par excellence.

These works measure between 80 and 100 centimetres in height. In each is a vase and in four cases some flowers are also lying near it on the table. There are no other still life subjects to be seen. Each bouquet of flowers is shown against a background of varying colours applied with flaky brush-strokes – sunflowers, mallows, chrysanthemums, jerusalem artichoke flowers and dahlias, all summer flowers, which indicates when they were painted. With the exception of the yellow ones Monet mainly chose blooms with matt, delicate colouring – above all in pink tones of varying intensity and shading. The general impression is of bright-coloured blossoms which are thrown into relief against the darker green leaves. In all these pictures both vase and flowers throw coloured shadows or reflections onto the polished surface of the table.

Two pictures stand out. The bunch of light pink mallow in the Courtauld Institute in London is perhaps the most impressionistic of the seven works. Everything dissolves into flecks and flakes of colour mainly created with tiny, irregular taps of the brush. Together with the comparatively restrained palette of complementary pastel shades – variations on the three primary colours of red, yellow and blue and mixtures of all three – a vibrant effect is produced through juxtaposing and simultaneously contrasting the colours, which at the time was a novelty in flower painting. In the second example of this impressionistic group, a vase with sunflowers in the New York Metropolitan Museum, this is all intensified through the use of stronger colours, predominantly the complementary red of the tablecloth with the yellow of the flowers, accompanied by the green of the leaves and the changing background shades of blue, and orange with hints of violet. This work may well have had an influence on van Gogh's sunflowers, painted eight years later in Arles, though less for its palette than for its iconography and form, and even then perhaps in an indirect way, difficult to reconstruct. Or is this similarity between Monet's strongly vivid and sinuous sunflowers and van Gogh's even more strongly inspired floral images just a coincidence? 'Van Gogh now informed Théo proudly that Gauguin considered the new still lifes with sunflowers he had painted for the Yellow House even finer than a similar work by Claude Monet . . . Van Gogh, however, seems to have been far from pleased with the painting.'[69] Did van Gogh not agree that his was better because he knew this picture of Monet's or because in general he laid greater value on the art of the leading Impressionist than on his own?

While these seven flower pieces from 1880 are all single pictures to be assessed individually, those painted in the following years are ornamental. Two extremely tall pictures of gladioli anticipate the decorative panels Monet painted later for Durand-Ruel. Two of the five flower pieces of 1882 are also very elongated, while the other three employ the simplified schematic of a flower vase against a calm, light background, which Monet may well have taken from the intimate flower paintings which Manet was producing at the same time, often with dark backgrounds. One cannot rule out the possibility that Monet was also influenced by other painters, such as Adolphe Monticelli or the 'flower specialists' Georges Jeannin and Ernest Quost, from whom van Gogh also learned much in his years in Paris.

The decorative character of two paintings of bunches of poppies in Chinese vases (1883), their blossom-bearing branches spread over the canvas, may like the mallow picture from the previous year have been inspired by Japanese woodcuts, which a few years later also had a strong effect on van Gogh. The door panels for Durand-Ruel's house represent in decorative form what Monet had already announced and achieved in his flower paintings. In 21 medium-sized to very tall paintings and 14 smaller but very wide ones, the painter presented all his subjects – jars and vases with flowers in bloom, as well as plants arranged in trailing garlands or strewn around. They are both a retrospective view of Monet's 'classical' flower paintings and a preview of the blossoms and tendrils in the Giverny water-garden.

One single latecomer from 1888 is at the same time a somewhat ponderous variation on his former compositional schema: on a large, horizontal canvas he set two bright, cylindrical Chinese vases diagonally on a white tablecloth in front of an orange to redbrown background. Yellow chrysanthemums in the left-hand vase stand beside whitey-pink ones in the right-hand vase. Here Monet ignites an explosion of colour supported by a flaky painting method: his last Impressionist flower painting.

INTERIORS AND EXTERIORS

The genre of interiors – depicting a room or part of a room – has an affinity with still life painting. It was particularly in his first 15 creative years that Monet worked in this field, doubtless in order to practise painting rooms. One of the earliest surviving examples (at 1.8 metres high one of the largest pictures from the first half of his career), depicting the corner of a studio, is a blend of still life and interior. On a red oriental carpet stands a dark-coloured, elaborately carved table placed in front of a wall decorated with tapestries and a picture. On and above the table are the painter's tools of paint-box, palette and brushes, with books and other furnishings, such as weapons hanging on the wall. It is lavish enough to be the studio of a Salon painter, which it probably was. This is Monet's only interior empty of people; all the later ones are enlivened with figures which are often even the principal subjects, while the room itself withdraws into the background.

Monet's interiors – as also his exteriors – are always spaces for people, so that the transition to portraits or scenic figure-paintings was easily made. Just as Monet needed specific motivation to inspire his portraits, still lifes and flower paintings, his interiors also resulted from opportunity or circumstance. It was about seven years after the studio painting that he produced any more interiors; in the winter of 1868-9 he painted two horizontal ones in Etretat, which are like studies, because of their limited size and sketchy execution. They are of people Monet knew, sitting or standing around a round table in the light of an oil lamp hanging from the ceiling. In one picture they are eating dinner and in the other they have just finished. Both works were probably preliminary studies for a very large picture – 2.3 metres – entitled *The Luncheon,* in which the scene is set in daylight in a dining room. Three women with a small child are sitting or standing around a table laid for lunch. This is in fact in strong contrast to the two evening studies, not only in its brightness but also in its meticulously realistic execution. It shows an affinity with Courbet and with the naturalism of writers like Zola or Goncourt, who demanded that modern life should be portrayed as it is. To us today it is hardly credible that this largely conventionally coloured and academically correctly painted picture should have been refused by the 1870 Salon, since it basically builds on Monet's first success in 1866 with *Camille or the Woman with a Green Dress.* The Frankfurt picture was undoubtedly another calculated career move. In his landscape pictures Monet's composition was by 1868/9 already more progressive.

Monet with a visitor in front of a fragment from "Dejeuner sur l'herbe" in his second studio

Another scarcely revolutionary painting is an interior portrait, showing Camille sitting in a daydream on a flowered sofa with a closed book in her hand, the scene lit by daylight coming through the blinds to the right of the picture. It is not very large. He painted it in London in the winter of 1870/1 and it was shown at the 1871 International Exhibition there.

Camille also appears in a much more interesting picture from 1873 – a spirited combination of interior and exterior. She is seen from inside, wearing a red headscarf and standing against a wintry backdrop, looking in through the glass panes of a terrace door. The viewer's gaze travels from inside to outside and the exterior scene seems to penetrate into the house. In the same year he painted this theme in reverse, with Camille looking out of the door into a summer scene full of bright flowers. Both pictures are painted in a noticeably lighter and more relaxed mood than the earlier examples. Two further interiors from 1875 are impressionistic: one shows Camille sitting at an embroidery frame in a kind of winter garden while the other is again very ingenious; one's gaze falls beyond

the sunlit façade of the Argenteuil house into the darker interior, which is framed in the background by a bright window half obscured with a blind. In the middle of the darkened room stands the graceful form of Monet's little son Jean, casting his elongated shadow over the parquet floor. These three Argenteuil interiors are in fact Monet's final pictures in this genre, which is therefore only represented in his œuvre by a small quantity of early works.

'Woman in a
Garden,' 1867.
Hermitage,
St Petersburg

However, Monet's figures occur more frequently in limited outdoor scenes, since he was after all mainly a landscape painter. His 1865 *Luncheon on the Grass* and the preliminary studies which go with it herald his resounding entry into the painting of exteriors. Both the title and spirit of this picture unmistakably refer to Manet's painting of the same name from 1863, which caused such a scandal. While the composition of the figures in Manet's work – in spite of its borrowing from the Italian high renaissance of Raphael – is clearer and bolder, showing a naked woman sitting with men in modern, street clothes in a woodland clearing, Monet's painting is more intricate and conventional, with elegant female figures in crinolines, while both by colour and composition the men are rendered inconspicuous. In this work, originally intended for the 1866 Salon but then abandoned, Monet declared his intention of presenting a group of figures in the open air together with their natural setting. He did not spare himself the effort of transporting the canvas, which was over six metres wide, to the Forest of Fontainebleau, in order to paint his models on the spot, lit by the sunlight filtering through the tops of the trees. Judging by the two surviving fragments and the general preliminary study (itself over 1.8 metres wide), Monet failed to convey the 'plein-air' impression that the figures had been painted out-of-doors in direct daylight, whereas the trees, especially in the upper half of the picture, make a completely new and charming effect.

After this failure Monet ventured on a second, similar composition. *Women in the Garden*, painted in 1866 and more than 2.5 metres high, portrays four women, sitting, standing and moving through the shrubbery in a sunny part of a garden. Here, too, the four meticulously delineated figures in very light clothing disrupt the artistically portrayed garden scene rather than harmonising with it. As in the fragments of his *Luncheon on the Grass,* Monet clung to this 'child of sorrows' into his old age, which does not alter the fact that here too he failed to fulfil his original intention.

Three further exteriors, painted in 1866/67 on the family property at Sainte-Adresse near Le Havre, are somewhat awkwardly executed. Two of them, painted in the Lecadres' garden, contain single figures which are too large to be incidental, too small and unimportant to be the principal subjects and not even skilfully positioned. Certainly at the age of 26 he was making a great effort to paint the festively decorated terrace above the sea of the Sainte-Adresse house, on which he clumsily arranged members of the family with their hats and sunshades. This picture, 1.3 metres wide, was actually the first of his paintings to reach one million dollars at auction and was acquired by the Metropolitan Museum in New York in 1967, but even this accolade does not enhance its artistic quality. It serves far more as a biographical document than as evidence of his ability as a painter. The far too geometrical composition, the muddled planes and the (for Monet) unusually bright colours prove that the painter was trying to achieve too much at once.

In comparison with those ambitious youthful works, the studies of women sitting in the sun, which Monet painted in 1870 on the beach at Trouville in the company of Boudin, are much more expressive because they are more spontaneous: Monet captures the essence and atmosphere of a summer scene of people on the beach through broad brushstrokes, swiftly and sometimes thickly applied. These are quick holiday snaps of carefree days before the outbreak of the Franco-Prussian War and also a timeless record of life at the seaside in general.

In the 1870s Monet was making similar attempts in the garden at Argenteuil, painting his little family and his guests – among them Manet – in the setting of a spring or summer garden in bloom, sometimes as incidental figures, sometimes equalling in importance the vegetation and sometimes again as the principal subjects, as in the 1873 picture *On the Bench*.

'Luncheon,' 1873. Musée d'Orsay, Paris. This is a scene in the garden of Monet's first house in Argenteuil; on the left, Jean, the artist's son is playing in the shadow of the table

The most famous of the five he painted in Argenteuil that year is the 2-metre wide garden scene *The Breakfast* In the foreground is a half-laid table, near which little Jean is playing on the ground with his bricks. On a bench to the right lie a bag and a sunshade. In the background two women are walking past in front of the house wall. Overhead a straw hat with black ribbons is hanging from a branch. Such a work (which is reminiscent of Renoir, in particular) became a model for countless decorative summer garden pictures by the Nabis, the legitimate but less talented French successors and heirs of the Impressionists. Above all Vuillard and Bonnard painted a great number of such pretty summer pictures of families in gardens, which in most cases only served as vehicles for delicate tones and decoratively structured surfaces.

In Monet's later exteriors the figures – mostly of women – are less individualised and almost incidental; with their light-coloured

clothes and open parasols they enliven the scenery – mostly of
fields of ripening corn or gardens in full bloom – and act as
colourful or formal counterpoises to the surrounding countryside.
From among this group of pictures three stand out – large-scale

'Camille Monet with a child in the painter's garden at Argenteuil,' 1875.
Museum of Fine Arts, Boston

paintings of white-clad women with parasols, the landscape being only indicated in the lower part of the canvas and by the sky in the background. The first of these, painted in 1875 (Washington), shows Camille with little Jean behind her and in 1886 came two companion versions (Paris), for which Suzanne Hoschedé posed as model. Although figures are under-represented in Monet's œuvre – in contrast to Renoir, who painted fewer landscapes – these three paintings exude the air and spirit of summer and the carefree atmosphere of a Sunday. Though they look like the quintessence of Impressionist painting they are, at least in Monet's case, in fact exceptions.

A small group of pictures painted in the late 1880s shows the Hoschedé daughters sitting or walking in the country near

Giverny and one of them, Blanche, painting at her easel. Most of these works are casually done and do not belong among Monet's strongest achievements.

The Hoschedé daughters also posed for a series of pictures produced in Giverny between 1887 and 1890, each of which depicts two or three girls in a punt or rowing boat on the Epte. The surprising thing about many of these pictures is their Japanese (and therefore unusual) composition with the boats cutting into the edge of the picture. Most of the girls in white summer dresses and hats are sketchily painted and faceless. While in the earlier versions of 1887 the atmospheric reflections in the water and the 'painting' factor dominate, in the two from 1890 the sinuous forms of the water plants stand out and provide a contrast to the more precisely and compactly painted boats and girls. For perhaps the last time we see disharmony in Monet's work, as he tries to represent all kinds of solid 'objects' – water, plants, boats and people – in a unified artistic context, that is, in one and the same style. This was Monet's problem from the start and may have been one of the main reasons why at a certain point in the middle of his life and work he started radically rejecting any motifs which 'disturbed' him, because they impeded the realisation of his artistic vision. Landscape alone offered him the means to develop an increasingly unified style.

Out of the two thousand-odd works in the catalogue, portraits, still lifes, flower paintings, interiors and exteriors comprise only a very small part of the oils, although about a dozen of them – particularly portraits and flower paintings – count among his important and individual works. Yet it must be acknowledged that Monet's non-landscapes feature in a surprisingly small minority in his œuvre, compared with more versatile painters like Cézanne and van Gogh, whose portraits and still life paintings comprise a notably higher proportion of their total output.

'Claude Monet painting at the edge of a wood,' by John Singer Sargent, 1887. Tate Gallery, London

LANDSCAPES

Landscape painting was Monet's personal domain. Though as a young man he applied himself to all the current genres (with the exception of historical and conceptual painting), by degrees he gave up most of them and in the second half of his life concentrated on landscapes.

While he started painting figures and still lifes in the conservative manner of the academic and fashionable painters of his time, his earliest landscapes are modelled on more progressive examples, including in particular the realist painters of the previous generation, among them Courbet, the Barbizon masters and the marine painters Boudin and Jongkind, all of whom impressed him with their vivid pictures. The method of painting directly en plein air in front of their subjects was common to all these artists and Monet remained fundamentally true to this practice, even though he later tended to complete his pictures in the studio, or for physical or conceptual reasons decided to paint at home. When questioned about this in later years, he usually tried to hide or deny it. He obviously feared for his good name as an plein-air painter, even though it had become public knowledge that he sometimes even worked from photographs. Basically he remained convinced that a faithful reproduction was only possible through direct contact with nature and the actual object. His Impressionist landscape-painter friends such as Pissarro, Sisley and Renoir shared this practice and conviction. The Barbizon painters worked only partly in en plein air: they usually created small studies of landscapes, so-called 'paysages intimes', direct from the subject, which was made possible by two circumstances – the invention in 1840 of easily transportable tubes of paint and simultaneously the arrival of the railway network. The Barbizon masters and the Impressionist who succeeded them liked to paint in and around places with railway stations, so that they did not have to carry their equipment too far on foot.

The Barbizon painters also normally completed their larger pictures in the studio, particularly those destined for exhibition, mostly having made smaller studies in oils out-of-doors. Seeing that they were therefore painted in a restful atmosphere, without pressure of time but only of competition and ambition, most of these studio pictures are too thoroughly elaborated, which makes them look lifeless. The plein-air studies, on the other hand, carry the stamp of direct impressions of nature with their incisive brushstrokes – sometimes thickly applied and 'alla prima' (without subsequent corrections) in a sort of artistic speed-writing, which can capture the essentials more than careful studio painting technique in old-master style. When painting spontaneously in the open air, the Barbizon painters captured momentary mood and atmosphere without photographic precision. Working swiftly in natural surroundings demanded a blending of forms, a summary technique which led away from mere images and prepared the way for the great revolution in painting: transcendence and symbolism.

While most of the Barbizon painters and their realist colleagues – Théodore Rousseau, Jules Dupré, Narcisse Diaz, Corot and Courbet – were painting both in the open air and in their studios, the landscape painter Charles-François Daubigny, living in Auvers to the north of Paris, was the first of his generation to work almost exclusively in the open air. As he preferred painting water scenes, he acquired a small house boat, in which he went painting on the Oise and the Seine. The roof of the boat – his 'open-air studio' – protected him and his pictures from bad weather and from the heat of the sun. It is not surprising that the young Monet admired Daubigny above all others and wanted to follow in his footsteps. They shared a love of 17th-century Dutch landscape painters and like them both Daubigny and Monet developed into masterly painters of water, snow and sky. Like his model in Auvers, Monet also painted from a covered boat on the Seine and Édouard Manet painted him doing so near Argenteuil. For his part, Daubigny early recognised in the young Monet a soul mate or possible successor and worked unselfishly in many different ways to help him.

Boudin and Jongkind, two painters who mainly worked on seascapes, were also masters of water and sky painting and their speciality clearly appealed to Monet, brought up as he was on the Normandy coast. All in all, therefore, a fortunate and beneficent constellation guided Monet on his way to becoming a landscape painter.

The earliest surviving landscape by Monet (painted at Rouelles, near Le Havre in 1858, when he was only 17 and still signing himself 'O. Monet') was clearly done under the supervision of Boudin. It shows a gently undulating countryside with a stream flowing through it, bushes, trees and the minor figure of a seated fisherman. This is an extraordinarily confident oil painting for a beginner. (Boudin may possibly have helped him.) Two smaller wooden panels from around 1860 are of the drab outskirts of a town and are decidedly simpler and less pretentious. From his early collaboration with Boudin hardly anything has survived, his first large landscape being *Farmyard in Normandy*, painted in 1863. In the foreground animals and small figures of people are grouped around a pond, and to the left are the farm buildings, framed to the side and behind by trees, like a scene by the Barbizon painters. It is a somewhat laboured and in some respects rather clumsy picture, painted in restrained natural colours, for under the pale blue sky all is green and brown.

In 1864 Monet's painting technique progressed and his palette became more contrasted, as we see in three landscapes painted in the Forest of Fontainebleau. In his own individual manner he was adapting what he had learnt from Théodore Rousseau and Corot. In the following year he painted several landscapes in the Forest near Chailly, the quality of which is absolutely equal to those of the Barbizon masters he so admired and who were also painting there. Among them two pictures, each 1.3 metres in width, stand out, one entitled *The Pavé de Chailly in the Forest of Fontainebleau*, of which he also painted a smaller version at a different time of year. The catalogue just describes this erroneously as a 'study'.[70] but it has a deeper significance: in contrast to the larger version the sky is cloudless and there are few leaves on the trees. This is the first evidence of Monet's later penchant for painting the same subject in differing weather conditions. The second of these large pictures depicts the so-called Bodmer Oak in the Forest of Fontainebleau, which should be studied in conjunction with his first large-scale picture, *Luncheon on the Grass* (1866), not only on account of the similar woodland scenery, but also because of the strongly contrasted colouring of the deep blue sky and sunlit green-gold foliage.

In Monet's early years the settings for his paintings fluctuated constantly between Paris, its rural surroundings and his hometown of Le Havre, near which he painted his marine pictures, the earliest survivors in this genre being eight seascapes of 1866, mostly of the open sea with sailing boats or the port of Honfleur. In the following years he devoted himself regularly to these themes and kept improving on his ways of painting them. Gradually his interest shifted from the man-made constructions of sailing boats to the natural scenery of the coastal region. For instance, masterpieces include a nocturnal seascape of 1866 and several pictures of the shore at Sainte-Adresse of 1867. Like Courbet, who also painted sea and shore on the Normandy coast, Monet applied white paint thickly for the crests of the waves and the clouds, using his colours to create expressive effects. The shades employed in these pictures are mostly lovely blends of blue, green and brown, based mainly on the natural colours. During the 1860s the tones in these early seascapes become brighter, creating a generally airier and lighter effect.

In the spring of 1867 Monet painted three views of Paris from the colonnades of the Louvre: the *Quai du Louvre*, the *Garden of the Princess* and a view of the Gothic church of Saint-Germain l'Auxerrois. All three are early Impressionist examples of urban and architectural painting, which throughout his life held

'Saint-Germain l'Auxerrois,' 1867.
Nationalgalerie. Berlin

a significant place among his landscapes. His 'teacher' Jongkind was also painting urban scenes as well as seascapes and he may have encouraged Monet to attempt something of the kind. The three views show the immediate vicinity of the Louvre with incidental pedestrians and coaches among freely applied splashes of the delicate green of early spring on the trees, in contrast to the more solid façades of the buildings, which are divided into areas of light and shade. Apart from one relatively sketchy view of the Pont Neuf, Monet only returned to such Parisian scenes some years later – for instance with two views of the bustling Boulevard des Capucines in 1873 and another four views of the Tuileries, painted in 1876 from the Rue de Rivoli apartment of his collector friend Victor Choquet. These two groups of scenes from the 1870s are already purely impressionistic in style – that is, with freely, sometimes very vehemently, applied brushstrokes and bright colours in varying tones to suggest light and shade.

'The Cart. Route in the snow, near Honfleur,' 1867. Musée d'Orsay, Paris

In the meantime, and later in life, Monet turned for preference to smaller, rural places for his landscapes with buildings – Bougival, Argenteuil, Vétheuil and later Giverny, returning repeatedly to the houses, churches and general views of these little towns and villages.

Like his older friend Pissarro, Monet must have been particularly fond of painting the entrance to a village or a road leading to or through a place. From 1864 on he discovered such subjects near the Normandy coast – for instance a spot on the road from Trouville to Honfleur which attracted him over and over again. Most of these pictures feature the Saint-Simon Inn either in the background or to one side, on the road which he painted repeatedly from both directions, horizontally and vertically. In the very tall canvases he created unusual compositions with exaggeratedly high trees, which almost anticipate some similar but much more expressively designed pictures by Chaim Soutine. Even in the winter Monet painted this scene, which obviously fascinated him – once in 1865 and then in 1867 in four different versions, all on horizontal canvases, portraying the scene in different weather and

at different times of day and always using different colours for the reflections off the snow. Apart from one, each version contains some small figures on the snow-covered road. The loveliest of this group of five shows a horse-drawn carriage passing over blue-shimmering snow.

Winter landscapes now became a speciality of Monet's. Near Bougival in 1867/68 he painted two different views of the snow-covered bank of the Seine with pack-ice on the river and in the following winter, beside five smaller views of the Seine bank, the wood and the entrance to the village, he created his 1.3-metre wide masterpiece of this genre, entitled *The Magpie*. In the middle of a snowy village scene with willow hedge, trees and a few village houses in the background, the bird sits on a fence. While the hedge which divides the foreground of the pictures is partly dark brown and casts light blue shadows on the white surface of the snow, the contrasts of light and dark melt into a pale, evocative mist. While being strongly related to the Barbizon painters in its lyrical approach to nature, this picture is an exception to Monet's otherwise completely unliterary output. Nevertheless, it is a masterly achievement.

Not only in winter but also in warmer seasons Monet often painted the banks of the Seine near Bougival. From four pictures, strongly reminiscent of Corot's delicately artistic creative manner, one unusual composition stands out because of its wild and crudely delineated, reddish, yellowish and grey-bluish evening sky, the free and masterly execution of which heralds his Dutch landscapes of 1871.

In the summer of 1869 Monet and Renoir painted several pictures of La Grenouillère, the favourite bathing-place of Parisians near Bougival. Once they sat – clearly side by side – in front of the same view, which they then painted apparently similarly but with very markedly characteristic differences. While Renoir, looking at the little island with its one tree standing in the water, mainly concentrated on details such as people's clothes and the scenery and assembled them in a not really unified picture, Monet restricted himself to essentials: the foreground and middle distance lying in shadow and the sunlight playing on the sparkling waves from the foreground to the background. The manner in which they painted the water alone shows the essential difference between the two Impressionists: where Renoir is hesitant and half-hearted, Monet's brushstrokes are decisive, almost brutal, like stab marks in white, pale blue and olive green, to suggest the play of light and shade and the reflection of the scene in the water. This evocation in colour of light, shade and reflection from now on became Monet's great theme.

The simple beach pictures which Monet painted on the shore at Trouville in 1870 and the exteriors with figures already mentioned stand out strongly from among his earlier series of coastal paintings. They reflect in very bright colours the beflagged, fashionable bathing resort with its summer atmosphere of light, water and sky and – brilliantly painted – that of its historical architecture and so embody a mixture of coastal and architectural pieces.

After a fallow period in London in 1870/71, in which he only produced two feeble views of Hyde Park and four admittedly better, but still only average, pictures of the Port, he burst out with a brilliant series of Dutch landscapes, their quality clearly enhanced by the results of his study of Turner and Constable, which had lain dormant during the winter. Water features in all 23 nature pieces painted in Zaandam; Monet was in his element among these scenes of coast and canal. He painted water, sailing boats, wind-mills, the charming, gaily painted cottages, the flat country between the waterways and the great expanses of partly sunny, partly cloudy sky above. With broad, stabbing brushstrokes he accentuated the red sails of the windmills, the reflections on the waves and the 'landscape' of the sky. The green, blue and red houses and the red sails of the windmills motivated him more strongly than ever before to apply pure colours.

Much of what Monet had absorbed around 1870 had already been started by his forerunners. Delacroix taught the Impressionist about the treatment of pure colours and the deliberate insertion of different shading into a picture, so that the effect could be enhanced with complementary and simultaneous contrasts. The renunciation of black – Manet still used this non-colour – and using colours to portray shadow had an effect on the colouristic lustre and charm of their pictures and their inimitable luminosity, which was unheard of at the time but today is taken for granted. The Impressionists of 1870 were pioneers. When Monet and Pissarro stood in front of Turner's and Constable's paintings in the London museums, they sensed not only a justification of their efforts so far but that the doors had swung back decisively to open up the path to their own impressionism. Constable's sensuous, *alla prima* painting, his concentration on how things looked at certain times of day – documented in his countless studies of clouds – and Turner's atmospheric veil of highly abstract colour truly laid a firm foundation stone for Impressionism. As a result, in Zaandam Monet's talent poured itself out in this series of Impressionist masterpieces. Now, at the age of 30, he was equipped to create his own style and the most important part of his output.

In the years at Argenteuil, between the end of 1871 and the beginning of 1878, what Monet had learned and tested in Bougival, London and Holland came to its full fruition. The water scenes he painted in that resort on the Seine have their place in art history as genuinely impressionistic pictures.

As he had done three years before at Bougival, Monet next turned to a substantial series of paintings of the Seine and of both its banks. While the trees change from the yellowish green of May to the deep chromium-oxide green of summer, the colours of the sky vary from a delicate pale blue through grey to the Neapolitan yellow of late afternoon. Perhaps in homage to Constable, the most varied cloud formations change from lyrical delicacy to dramatic plasticity. This very beautiful group of riverside pictures, faintly reminiscent of Courbet and Corot (Monet worked on four drafts for each one), reach their peak in a painting of the harbour at

Argenteuil, the mood of which is entirely determined by the main contrast of the green of nature with the blue of sky and water, together with a few additional minor reddish or greenish accents. It is distinguished from the other, rather more peaceful, riverside pictures by its lively structure of clouds, the striped shadows of trees in the foreground and the details in the middle distance and background; it already heralds the future developments in his landscape painting. A lively surface, achieved through freely applied brushstrokes, increasingly became a fundamental principle of Impressionism – also in the cases of Pissarro and Sisley, the other two significant landscape painters in this group of fellow-artists.

In the course of the summer of 1872 Monet turned to the sailing boats in the Argenteuil yacht basin and continued in miniature what he had started some years previously in Honfleur, Fécamp and Etretat: illustrating boats or ships, with and without sails, with vertical masts and a variety of triangular sails, their floating reflections in the water artistically curved and disintegrating like abstract dream images. Probably the loveliest of this group is the bright summer scene, radiant with complementary contrasts – red for houses, green for vegetation, primary yellow for sails and pale blue for sky and water. Apart from the use of primary colours, the most important thing about a picture like this is the strongly simplified and taut composition of shapes with those broad, squared-off strokes – especially for the reflections in the water – which first featured in *La Grenouillère* and in Zaandam and had now became a principle of Monet's brushwork technique.

In that summer of 1872 Monet also painted several sea pictures of large sailing ships on the broader reaches of the Seine near Rouen. Here he strongly emphasised the ships and relegated the riverbank to the background. He painted two more pictures in Rouen the following summer, after completing six similar seascapes in Le Havre (among them a nocturnal view), of which one is the most evocative and progressive, due to its rough outlines, misty haziness and a palette restricted to the complementary contrast of orange and blue. When it was exhibited in 1874 he called it (probably without any thought of a programme) *Impression, Sunrise.* The antagonistic leading critic Albert Wolff then turned this title into a collective term 'impressionism' which he intended to be sarcastic and dismissive but which was eventually embraced by those he was aiming at as a title of honour and established itself in the terminology of art history. *Impression, Sunrise* is in fact the most strongly and unambiguously 'impressionist' picture so far, not only by Monet but by anyone in the group; everything in it is just sketchily hinted at. The composition – insofar as one can use the term here – consists of dashes and strokes of paint and amorphous areas, which taken together suggest a hazy sunrise. With sparing, basically lapidary, means he achieved the maximum atmospheric effect and communication of mood.

While producing some more river and harbour pictures in varying compositions and colours during the following years, Monet was turning significantly to other subjects, which he found in his home environment and elsewhere. Around Argenteuil he was now also painting open views of the countryside, of orchards with apple trees in blossom or of meadows and cornfields. The most beautiful of these comes from 1873 and shows a field of red poppies, through which two women and two children are walking in their Sunday best. Renoir painted similar subjects but any comparison shows up the differences more than the impressionistic similarities; as in his *Grenouillère* painting, Renoir loses himself in detail, which makes his interpretation less unified. In Monet's case, however, everything holds together in a masterly artistic blend; also, his composition is in no way haphazard or arbitrary – terms which superficial critics of Impressionist pictures have generally used to denigrate it ever since. In Monet's 1873 field of poppies there is something worth noting, which comes to the fore in the later serial paintings of Giverny: the artist is increasingly employing colour as a tool of his composition, to make deliberate accents which significantly stabilise the balance of a picture's texture and can thus compensate for a certain lack of constructive draughtsmanship. In this picture we see this clearly, in the transferring of the bright, vermilion red poppies almost entirely to the left side of the canvas, while on the right side the two figures in the foreground create a formal balance with the vivid colours on the left. The tall tree on the horizon and the more varied textures of the sky on the left form a basically asymmetrical scheme, customary in the western principle of the 'golden cut', which Monet had encountered in Japanese woodcuts, though in more incisive form.

From 1873 on Monet was painting various views of his garden at Argenteuil, with and without figures, as well as several pictures of the centre of the village and of houses on the outskirts. He had already noted the architectural features of his new hometown in 1872 and in numerous pictures over the following years painted both the road and railway bridges over the Seine. In 1874 especially, after his second visit to Holland at the beginning of the year, when he painted some architectural views and three pictures with railway bridges in Amsterdam, he created a whole series of masterly renditions of the two Argenteuil bridges – perhaps his most important works in that town. While in some of these pictures the bridges are arranged almost or entirely parallel to the frame – another principle of iconography and form he knew from coloured Japanese woodcuts – his portrayals of them on the diagonal, occupying more of the canvas, are probably the more convincing and evocative.

'Poppy field near Argenteuil,' 1873. Musée d'Orsay, Paris

'Outside view of Saint-Lazare Railway Station on the arrival of a train,'
1877. Private Collection

Monet's two main works in this manner each exist in two
different forms. While both versions of the road bridge going
diagonally from the right into the depths of the canvas on the
left differ, particularly in the foreground, in the number of sailing
boats at anchor and the presence or absence of greenery on the
bank, the composition of the two large pictures of the railway
bridge at an angle – apart from a sailing boat which is missing
from one of them – is more or less identical. What has changed
is the light, and with it the shadow on the subject; the version in
Philadelphia is bathed in sunlight with strong contrasts of light

and shade and more intensely colourful radiance, while the Paris version depicts a gloomy day with little contrast and also gives the impression of a more subdued palette. In a pair of paintings so varied in weather and atmosphere one can see in retrospect the germ of Monet's later serial paintings, which mainly concentrate on such differences in light.

Though in the suburban studies of his early period man-made objects like factory chimneys had already featured, he was using such things more in the 1870s. He did not just paint the engineering element of a bridge but also emphasised that of the steam train puffing across it. Other painters of his circle, such as Pissarro and Cézanne, had already put railway trains in their pictures. They were all following the demands of contemporary naturalistic writers not to omit everyday elements of modern life from painting, but on the contrary to include them deliberately. There was another important inspiration behind Monet's railway pictures: in London in 1870/71 he had seen Turner's 1844 painting *Rain, Steam and Speed – the Great Western Railway*, which shows a locomotive with coaches only roughly indicated crossing a (diagonal!) bridge. It was not only the artistic freedom of Turner's brightly coloured splashes of light and veils of mist, but also giving the picture a title which puts a name to the atmosphere, which must have made a great impression on Monet, however much he later tried to deny it and play it down!

The 1874 pictures of railway bridges, which Van Gogh took as models for his 1887 painting *The Railway Bridge of Asnières*,[71] are indisputably indebted to the Turner picture Monet had seen four years before. Having painted several pictures near the Argenteuil railway station in 1872 and 1875, in 1877 he embarked boldly on a new iconographic course with a dozen pictures painted in the Gare Saint-Lazare. In 1873 Manet had painted *The Railway* in that station. In it the industrial world is almost entirely smothered in steam and all one sees are some figures in the foreground.

'Waterloo Bridge, grey sky,' 1899-1901.
Ordrupgaardsamlingen, Copenhagen

Gustave Caillebotte also painted railways in 1876 at the Pont des Arts but in his picture, too, genre figures in modern dress take precedence over the technical elements. Not so with Monet, who only put small figures in outline into his Saint-Lazare pictures. His main theme is the world of locomotives belching steam among the lines and bridges, both in and outside the station building. Unlike his later serial paintings, Monet chose a different, independent composition for each of the 12 pictures. In this cycle he rendered visible in artistic terms the ambience of a city railway station. Much of it is only fragmentary and hinted at, and some things are veiled in steam and smoke. In most of the pictures typical Parisian houses can be seen in the background, sometimes bathed in sunlight and sometimes in sombre shadow. In these paintings he seems to have been most attracted by juxtaposing the solid, physical forms of locomotives and buildings with amorphous, atmospheric elements of smoke, light and shade. He succeeds in managing the colours of this scene, which at first glance seem to be just shades of grey, by using delicately graded tones of blue, violet and ochre. This railway cycle confounds a widespread prejudice against the Impressionists, according to which they *exclusively* painted the world in its Sunday best. Here the technical workaday business of a metropolis is translated into artistic snapshots.

After a break of over five years, Monet painted several winter landscapes around Argenteuil in the 1870s, prompted perhaps by his friends Pissarro and Sisley, who were living in the neighbourhood, but in 1876 he changed to a different theme. For the interior of the Hoschedés' country house at Montgeron he painted a set of very large-scale decorative panels of themes from their gardens, as well as some views of the river. Four were only mediocre but the fifth, an almost square panel measuring 1.72 x 1.75 metres, is a masterpiece. It features white turkeys on a shady sloping meadow with the house framed by trees in the background. The white of the birds, varied with bluish and yellowish tones, subtly deviates from the predominant complementary contrast of the red of the birds' heads and the dusty pink of the house front against the green of grass and trees. The subject in itself is worth noting, for the Impressionists who specialised in landscapes rarely chose animals or birds as their main figures. Monet, who surprised everyone with his pictures of the Gare Saint-Lazare in the following year, was already showing his unconventionality.

After painting a series of four views of the banks of the Seine near Argenteuil from the same spot in 1877 – another precursor of his later series – he turned in the following year to the river nearer Paris, on the so-called Ile de la Grande Jatte near Asnières, which Georges Seurat's great pointillist painting made famous about a decade later. In Asnières Monet was not only creating riverside views in compositions comparable to those from Bougival and Argenteuil, but also some pictures of the brushwood and undergrowth by the river – a subject which van Gogh endeavoured to master in numerous oil paintings nine years later. By hinting at the foliage behind the river and on the far bank through applying tiny, delicate dabs of paint, Monet made it look like filigree network; this decorative trellis-work in the foreground was inspired by Japanese woodcuts.

On 30 June 1878, having painted several insignificant pictures in the Parc Monceau in Paris in the spring, Monet felt drawn to portray the centre of the city decked out in bunting for the National Day. He made two vertical pictures of Rue Montorgueil and Rue Saint-Denis decorated in the tricolour. Everything is done in blue, white and red brushstrokes and dabs of paint – the crowds below in the street, the banners hanging from the house fronts, the construction of the walls and even the bright sky. The dizzy impression given by the colours applies to the whole picture; its content and its manner of giving the visible appearance of a festival are both spontaneous and impressively symbolic.

Monet was painting places apart from Argenteuil increasingly frequently – an indication that he had exhausted his subjects in and around the town itself. In the next years it was Vétheuil and its environs, further downstream, which became to him what Argenteuil had been for some five years. Immediately on his first exploratory visit he had painted one horizontal and one vertical view of the church there, two splendid architectural pieces in sparse brushwork, which lets the bright background shine through. Once he had settled in Vétheuil with his large family, he immediately produced a considerable number of water scenes from the riverbank and from his boat – a subject which he varied repeatedly over the next years. He also liked to paint Vétheuil from Lavacourt on the opposite bank, as a group of houses clustered around the tall church by the river and reflected in the water.

The severe icy conditions of the winter of 1879/80 served him as an incentive to paint in great haste a substantial series of winter scenes of the Seine covered with blocks of ice and the silvery, misty bank. Monet varied the delicate, pale colour values, mingling them with the white of snow and ice. Although most of these pictures are differently composed, a study of the cycle as a whole gives almost the same effect as do his later serial pictures.

Nowhere did Monet paint so many winter landscapes as in Vétheuil. He even repeatedly reproduced the road leading into the town, on which his house lay, in the splendour of pastel-shaded snow. He also painted in Lavacourt in winter and in summer, and in warmer weather roamed around the area in search of subjects. He painted fruit trees in blossom and bearing fruit, applying his paint in a mixture of different coloured spots and comma-shaped strokes. Such pictures of Monet's, in which some rustic buildings also appear in the hollows, are most closely related to Pissarro's works.

Having painted the meadows and fields of poppies around Vétheuil in different ways, he repeatedly returned to the Seine to capture it afresh in other ways, sometimes with small, wooded islands in the foreground and behind them the riverbank with the houses of Lavacourt, or even new views of Vétheuil reflected in the water. However he never tired of ringing the changes on his standard view of Vétheuil and was now inserting virtuoso brushstrokes and employing a subtle palette, which could suggest both strongly contrasted summer colours and the more muted tones of overcast weather. Like a keyboard player, he was now the virtuoso master of the whole gamut of impressionist technique.

Perhaps because he had painted hardly anything but the region around Vétheuil for two years, Monet set off in 1880 on some major travels. The first took him once again to the Normandy coast, where in the next few years he mainly devoted himself to the steep coastline, the beaches and the sea. Although he had been creating impressive seascapes since the 1860s, only now came his real masterpieces in this genre. In Fécamp and Dieppe, particularly in 1881 and 1882, with a delicacy of style and a soft, light-toned palette reminiscent of Turner he painted a large number of astonishing reproductions of the coastal cliffs of his native Normandy, always varying the colours and viewing them in different ways. The whole cycle reached its climax in 1882 in a significant series of coastal landscapes of stunningly high quality, painted in the neighbourhood of Pourville. His painting of the church of Varengeville at sunset represents both progress and break-through in his use of colour: the sky is tinted a glistening lemon yellow, in front of which on the upper left edge of the picture the church stands out in silhouette above a blue-green sloping meadow, covered in the right foreground with bushes varying in colour from orange to olive green, out of which two dark green trees stretch up into the dominant yellow of the sky. This is a forerunner of the exciting strong colours in which van Gogh was painting only six years later in Arles — at the opposite, southern tip of France.

In Varengeville Monet often painted the customs officer's cottage on the high, angular cliffs in various manners, and behind it a violet, blue, greenish or yellowish sea stretching to a blurred, misty horizon. Besides executing some more delicate views of the shore, he was continually striving for the ultimate in spontaneity, by vigorously spreading his glowing colours with broad, thickly applied brushstrokes which he left unaltered. A brilliant example of such powerful original work is another portrayal of the church at Varengeville, this time seen from the shore, rising high and small into the blue and white sky above steep cliffs constructed with wild, exuberant colours. Such a picture is another example of the affinity between Monet's and van Gogh's compositions.

In Etretat, where Corot, Courbet, Delacroix and others before him had painted the massive cliffs, Monet produced in 1883 a series of pictures of the same subject in different weather conditions and at different times of day – with reflections or dramatic wave patterns and eventually also with boats on the beach as part of the composition. These boats may have helped to inspire van Gogh's famous *Boats on the Beach*, painted in Arles or Les Saintes-Maries.[72] In 1883 Monet also twice painted the rocky entrance to the Manneport looking like the massive pier of a bridge above raging seas.

Boats appear in two of the only three surviving pictures painted by Monet in 1882 in his temporary house in Poissy, which never felt like home to him or provided him with artistic inspiration. The boats are viewed from above, with fishermen sitting or standing in them. In the two pictures there is no horizon and the water has the main role, with glittering greens and yellows merging into shades of red. This is a foretaste of what was to become the virtually exclusive object of Monet's interest in later life: reflections of the actual world on the surface of water, as it captures light and throws back colours.

Monet's travels in the 1880s took him from the north to the south of France and thus to two completely different types of landscape and climate. Between 1880 and 1882 he repeatedly returned to the subjects and artistic challenges awaiting him on the Normandy coast and created an important yield of seascapes, both in quantity and quality, which he brought home to work on or to retouch. Then in the winter of 1883/84 on his first visit to the south he discovered more coastal regions but with completely different, partly tropical vegetation and above all a different world of colour under the stronger sunlight. In his letters from Bordighera he keeps mentioning that he needs to get acclimatised to the intensive colours, to examine himself and modify his palette, and this in spite of the fact that already in 1882 in Varengeville he had employed bold, pure tones, in anticipation of the southern landscapes. On 11 March 1884 he wrote to Durand-Ruel: *It may well cause an outcry among the enemies of blue and pink, but it's precisely that brilliance, that magical light which I am trying to render, and those who have never seen this country or who have not looked at it properly, will complain, I'm sure, that it's unrealistic, although I am quite a bit below the {usual} tone: everything here is dove-blue shading to violet and flaming punch-pink. It's wonderful and the landscape grows lovelier every day, and I'm enchanted with this country.*[73] Van Gogh wrote something similar four years later from Arles in the south of France.

In and around Bordighera Monet painted in all four dozen splendid landscapes. These views of the Riviera and the Côte d'Azur, of gardens with palm trees, hilltop villages and olive groves, not only widened his pictorial sphere but also the range of iconography of French Impressionism. The younger Post-Impressionists – especially van Gogh and Paul Signac – created their most important works in the South of France a few years after Monet. Only his contemporary, the Post-Impressionist Cézanne who came from this region and spent most of his life there, had painted his pictures of this scenery before Monet. Perhaps it was a lucky chance that

Renoir and Monet visited their fellow-student Cézanne in L'Estaque at the end of 1883. The sight of Cézanne's pictures of Provence may possibly have inspired Monet to try and paint this scenery for himself.

Monet rose brilliantly to this artistic challenge. Among the pictures he painted in Bordighera are some of his most beautiful landscapes of all: the many different views of the little town, in a composition which sparkles with pure, clear, glowing colours, were executed with even, rhythmic, free strokes and dabs of the brush. This technique, together with the serpentine lines of the tree trunks in the foreground, as well as the predominant contrasts of green and different shades of red, are striking forerunners of van Gogh's Provençale landscapes. The Dutchman may have seen these pictures of Monet's in Paris in 1886 or 1887.

Various views from Signor Moreno's garden evoke what he had learnt from Turner. When in the midst of the southern vegetation villas and distant mountains dissolve in scintillating light – just suggested by the substance and shades of paint – and in air which vibrates, Monet is proving that he and 'his' Impressionism have now reached an artistic apogee, on the very limits of creating in a figurative painting an impression of a tangible, discernible environment and communicating it to the viewer.

Van Gogh, arriving on the artistic scene a few years later, blazed a new trail towards 'expression'. How he continued this and simultaneously overtook what Monet had achieved can be clearly seen when one compares the Dutchman's 1889 pictures of olive groves at Saint-Rémy with Monet's works from Bordighera in 1884. Monet's deliberately recognisable depiction of the natural 'movement' in the shapes of the trees is completely transformed by van Gogh into a 'systematic' network of curving brushstrokes which turn the olive trees into animated, speaking, symbolic living beings. Here Monet's 'impressive' and van Gogh's 'expressive' art are closely related to each other, without however overlapping. Especially in his technique and use of colour, Van Gogh's expressive style certainly derives from Monet's Impressionism, among other influences.

When van Gogh first arrived in Arles four years later at the beginning of 1888, Monet was staying on the Mediterranean coast for the second time, this time only on the French Côte d'Azur, where he was now mainly painting coastal landscapes, always including the water whose constantly changing forms and colours continually challenged and fascinated him afresh. Among the 40 landscapes he painted in and around Antibes are many views of the town seen from different viewpoints and in different ways, with its fortifications rising like a Turneresque mirage out of air which is sometimes misty and sometimes gleams in the sunlight above the sea and in front of the mountains and sky. Other reproductions show the bay without Antibes but instead, to balance the shore area floating distantly in the haze, a strip of greenery in the foreground – compositions reminiscent of Ferdinand Hodler's later views of Lake Geneva. Besides some views of cliffs and beach, the forms of which Monet could most easily relate to from his coastal landscapes of Normandy and Brittany, he also created a series of pictures of pines on Cap d'Antibes, choosing the Japanese method of a trellis-like foreground of tree trunks, through which the sea in the middle distance and the far, hilly shore can be seen. The stronger 'constructivism' in these compositions could be a development on what he had seen of Cézanne's work. Their clearly defined lines anyway make these paintings relatively uncharacteristic – even unusual – for Monet, who normally blended the subjects in his pictures into each other, and are generally somewhat weaker than the rest of the work he did around Antibes.

The most important result of these two long visits to the Mediterranean coast concerned colour; from now on Monet was to be much bolder with his palette. On his third visit to Holland in the spring of 1886 between the two journeys to the south, when van Gogh had just left for Paris, Monet painted near Leyden and Haarlem four horizontal pictures of tulip fields with windmills or farmhouses in the background. More than four decades later, when he was in his 80s, he recalled the moving artistic experiences of this visit: *Tulips are beautiful but impossible to render. When I saw that, I told myself that painting couldn't manage it. But then I had twelve successive days of almost unvarying weather; what luck! You don't like tulip fields, you find them too uniform? I love them, and when they cut the blooms in flower and pile them up, and you suddenly make out, on the little canals, dabs of yellow in the blue shimmer of the sky, like rafts of colour . . .* [74] He saw not only 'dabs of yellow', but also painted red tones into his skies – and not only in the pictures from this visit!

How much the Impressionists were already diverging artistically at that time is demonstrated by Pissarro's revealing criticism of one of these Dutch pictures, which he saw in a Paris exhibition in the company of an acquaintance, Félix Bracquemond. By then Pissarro was a convinced pointillist and on 15 May 1887 wrote to his son Lucien: 'He [Bracquemond] has also noticed the crude execution of certain paintings by Monet, a Dutch canvas on which the paint is plastered in such thick relief that it adds an artificial light to the canvas (you can't imagine how disagreeable I find it) and what is more, with a blank sky swept clean; no, I cannot accept this way of understanding art.' [75] Just by the artistic technique of juxtaposing thickly painted tulip fields in the foreground with soft, flat strokes to make up the delicate area of sky, in this picture (as in some others) Monet was able to convey convincingly the feeling of the difference in consistency of translucent air and tangible, material objects. Van Gogh learnt such stylistic ideas from Monet, among others. The critical Pissarro, when some years later pointillism had become too systematic, inexpressive and time-consuming for him, returned 'repentantly' to the Impressionist camp.

In the late summer of 1886 Monet settled on the very wild, rocky, jagged coast of the Breton island of Belle-Ile, and there created some more landscapes painted very thickly like reliefs. By the time he left again on 25 November he had painted 38 canvases in all, of which 35 represent the cliffs surrounded by foaming sea or steep rocky configurations rising out of the water. His letters testify to the way in which he captured the battle of the elements on the spot. He wrote to Durand-Ruel: *. . . but the sea is inimitably beautiful and accompanied by fantastic rocks. Moreover, the place is called 'The wild sea.' . . . I'm fascinated by this sinister region, above all because it takes me beyond my normal limits; I must admit I am having to really punish myself in order to render this gloomy and fearful atmosphere.*[76]

On 11 October he wrote to his painter friend Caillebotte: *As for me, I've been here a month and am working hard. I'm in a magnificent, wild district: a mighty accumulation of rocks and a sea whose colours are incredible. Yes, I'm very enthusiastic, although I have a lot of trouble because I was used to painting on the Channel coast, and I naturally had a form of routine. But the ocean is quite another matter.* It was just this divergence from his 'routine' which makes the works he did on Belle-Ile so special. On 30 October he wrote to Alice about the ocean which struck him as so novel: *. . . In short, I'm mad about it, but I'm well aware that, in order to paint it really well, one has to see it every day, at every hour and from the same spot, in order to understand its life.*[77] Every day he set off, in wind and storm, to transfer onto canvas what he saw on Belle-Ile. As in the paintings he made in Bordighera, Monet here approached very near to van Gogh's expressionist style, through the vigour of his spontaneous brushstrokes and the subtleties of contiguous yet separate flecks of colour. Also as with van Gogh, one can tell that where the artist has the requisite receptiveness and disposition, the special character of scenery can effect not only choice of colour but also technique: the savagery and ruggedness of nature in the raw inspired Monet to a corresponding style of painting, which endowed his works with a new dimension, also to be found in his later serial paintings.

As he grew older, Monet's strenuous painting trips became rarer. Before and around 1900 he did make a few nostalgic excursions to earlier sites such as Vétheuil and Etretat, but brought back hardly any pictures of outstanding quality, for he was already too taken up with his idea for serial works to be able or want to create convincing single works which would stand on their own. On the visit he paid to Norway at the beginning of 1895 to paint winter landscapes his work was hampered by adverse circumstances. Most of what he painted there already belongs to his late genre of serial pictures. Only a view of a red-painted farmhouse set in snow which shimmers with green, bluish and violet tones, painted with broad, flat brushstrokes, can be regarded as a self-contained single work.

On his remaining foreign travels, to London around the turn of the century and finally to Venice in 1908, serial pictures took up almost all of his time, though in Venice he did also produce three single works: a view of the Doge's Palace and two oil sketches – one of a red palace and one of a gondola.

Between these long, important painting trips in the 1880s, Monet kept returning to the countryside around Giverny, where he had settled in 1883. He painted the stream and banks of the Seine and of its tributary the Epte, and also Vernon on the left bank of the main river whose church, towering over the surrounding the houses and trees, presumably reminded him of Vétheuil. In 1884 he was working on the left bank of the Seine near Jeufosse, as we know from a quantity of different views of the river. From 1885 he also returned to painting winter landscapes around Giverny or nearby Port Villez, and painted the village of Falaise in both summer and winter. These pictures with village roof-scapes resemble some of Pissarro's works.

Also reminiscent of his older companion in both composition and execution are the two versions of the picture *The Church at Bennecourt*, which is a rare example of his making architecture the focus of a picture, in this case the arrangement of village buildings around and in front of the Gothic church. The pale brown path leading to the church is outlined in an abstract pattern of dark indigo shadows thrown by the houses on the right. Only two small trees, a patch of grass on the left and a narrow strip of green on the horizon pay tribute to organic nature. Such a picture from his middle period shows that this most important of the Impressionists was also a virtuoso master of painting man-made objects like architectural complexes, even though he used this talent much too little, in favour of the 'amorphous' natural landscapes which constitute by far the greater part of his œuvre. Such a picture, which carefully balances individual components and format, contradicts the myth that weakness in composition had become a characteristic of the works of Monet and the other Impressionists. The asymmetric arrangement of the objects and the façade of one of the houses cut sharply into the right-hand edge of the picture also show that Monet had not only studied but absorbed the pictorial cut-outs of the Japanese.

The stage for Monet's art was not only buildings and water but also, as he roamed around the environs of Giverny, flowering meadows and fields of poppies or of ripening or harvested corn, of which he made single paintings or small, varied series. Around Giverny he also painted mixed landscapes consisting of both fields and groups of trees or bushes, the most beautiful examples of these themes being those dating from 1887. Lovely summer scenes are frequently enlivened with minor figures with straw hats or parasols, standing in fields of flowers. Although, as on Belle-Ile, he was already using coarser, thicker and wilder brushstrokes, these summer scenes were painted with delicate, varied dabs of paint in front of mostly flat expanses of pale blue sky. Accents of yellow, red and green – sometimes complementary – are most frequently to be found in the lower halves of the pictures, which are in general more animated. Together with some views of orchards in blossom – also containing unimportant figures – these happy pictures of smiling seasons have become a hallmark of Impressionist landscape art. In their bright, pure colours, sensitive, flocculent execution and not least in their cheerful subjects, they convey something of Monet's love for and affinity with nature and his search for fulfilment in his creativity.

IMPRESSIONISM

With the shimmering water pictures from the Grenouillère at Bougival of September 1869, the bright beach views of Trouville the following summer and the strongly coloured, powerfully constructed Zaandam pictures of 1871, Monet had reached a stylistic level which can be defined as true Impressionism. He employed the next two decades in exploring the scope of the innovative style he had now found and which both critics and public had at first dismissed. He applied himself in practical ways to producing a rich collection of single pictures on a variety of subjects, developing a certain consistency of form, technique and colour and experimenting with the capacity, range and other possibilities of this new style. Unlike any of his fellow-painters, he worked in a masterly and methodical way until he reached a point beyond which his previous companions could only follow him to a limited extent or not at all. When in the second half of his artistic career he turned to serial painting, he even went beyond the boundaries of his own impressionist principles and for the second time in his life entered new territory in which he was working until his death, committed and completely on his own.

Impressionism, originally intended as a derisive epithet, was eventually accepted as an honourable title by its adherents. In writings on art history it has also been used widely and carelessly as a catchword to be applied to everything and nothing. Even though in old age some of the Impressionists distanced themselves from this terminological stereotype, the stylistic definition still really accurately embraces – better than so many other erroneous terms such as 'mannerism' or 'abstraction' – what it was basically intended to describe from the start and what distinguished the essential element in the Impressionist pictures of Monet, Pissarro and Sisley, as well as to a limited extent also those of other contemporaries: the evocation of a spontaneous moment, the rendition of an impression captured on canvas in front of the subject. As we have already particularly seen in Monet's figure paintings but also in his still lifes, people and objects – that is, firmly delineated corporeal phenomena – are only relatively well suited to the impressionist style, that is, to transferring onto canvas a charm and magic which is atmospheric and therefore barely tangible in concrete terms. Even in his landscapes Monet had always had to struggle with the fleeting nature of different seasons and times of day, on which the relationships of light and therefore also the colours of natural objects depend. This led perforce to a swift, spontaneous manner of painting, as otherwise the momentary aspect of the subject could not be captured on canvas. In later life Monet's whole obsession and concern were to seize on *immediacy* and record it in his pictures – a paradoxical, and in the final analysis useless, struggle, which 20th-century colour films were able to realise much more consistently and lastingly.

Immediacy: Monet and his impressionist friends attempted to realise in their paintings the words in which Goethe's Faust addressed the moment: 'Stay awhile, you are so lovely', but in the event they only approached this ideal, creating approximations which were nevertheless in many cases superb examples of artistic achievement. Impressionist pictures are often reproached with being too superficial, with only showing the outward appearance and the brief moment, and not the being, the essence, the inner life of what they portray. In spite of all the truth contained in this assessment, which can be regarded as entirely positive, it should be set against the whole spectrum of innovation, with which this style has revolutionised and revived the art of painting and from which artists are profiting to this day.

This innovation actually consists in liberating paint, giving it its own validity in a picture, turning away from those greys and browns and much too sombre tones which were academically obligatory up to the middle of the 19th-century and beyond. From the use of free, autonomous brushstrokes there emerged the capacity to move away from photographic or imitative images of natural subjects. Cézanne's statement that art is 'a harmony parallel to nature'[78] was based on the Impressionists, and specifically on Monet. From that point on a painted picture was no longer a reproduction or a copy but an image in its own right, showing and expressing something representative and symbolic; his main concern was no longer solid trees in blossom but the evocation of blossoming itself, no longer a recognisable stretch of the Seine but the evocation of water itself. From here it was only a step – albeit an important one – to expressive art and so to Expressionism itself. When van Gogh in his maturity stressed that Impressionism was a useful transitional stage on the road to more distant objectives, he meant above all technical ability and deployment of colour, which he too, under the influence of the Impressionists, had acquired in Paris on his way to Arles. Even Cézanne passed through Impressionism and owed it a debt of gratitude. He and van Gogh – each in his own, inimitable manner – passed beyond Impressionism. Monet valued the art of these two Post-Impressionists, particularly Cézanne, and was reluctant to have his own works exhibited alongside Cézanne's but Monet is in fact the only Impressionist who has no need to fear comparison with Cézanne and van Gogh. The superb quality of his art, his assurance and delicacy in handling his colours, his choice and unique renditions of landscapes assure him a place among the very greatest painters in history.

The Serial Pictures:
Failure at the highest level

For more than two decades Monet had been painting out-of-doors, in accordance with his 'impressionistic' principle, striving to capture atmosphere, seasons and the tangible effect of light and to select the necessary palette for each subject. When he was away from home, sudden changes of weather or bad conditions for days on end could hinder, prevent or interrupt the work he had embarked on, so in his latter years he changed to a different way of working, which allowed him to react appropriately to the vagaries of the weather. He carried several canvases with him (in increasing numbers as the years went by), on which he started different pictures at different times of day and in different weather conditions, and worked on them again when the light and colour were right. It was then disastrous for him when the weather changed completely – for instance, when dull, rainy days followed a sunny period. In such cases he could either break off his work in the open air and take the pictures home to finish from memory, or else stay where he was and either scratch away the paint he had already applied or paint over it in accordance with the new conditions.

Although it was initially unintentional, out of this method he gradually developed whole series of pictures to portray a scene in different conditions and at different seasons of the year. Over and over again in despair he failed in his quest for the 'true' momentary impression, in spite of all his efforts to capture an instant in a picture which he had had to work on for far longer than its duration. So he was continually seeking the lost moment, the visual experience which had already passed. In comparison with his impressionist colleagues Monet was the most uncompromising and persistent in the pursuit of this objective. It became *the* obsession of his life. To it he subordinated everything – health, wealth and material gain and eventually even the originality and idiosyncrasy of his individual pictures. At the age of about 50 he eventually saw that the only possibility of even approaching his goal was to develop his unique pictorial invention into larger and larger series. In his main concentration on light and colour – that is, on atmosphere – Monet was almost compelled to reject the enlivening irregularity and unique qualities of his single compositions. The serial routine simplified and condensed the single subject, robbed it of its expressive detail and viewed it superficially in both senses. The more delicate and refined his treatment of the colours and his brushwork technique became, the more insignificant, flat and purely decorative the actual portrayal of the subject turned out to be.

Cézanne's aphorism that Monet was an eye is more than an apposite bon mot. Monet, more intensively perhaps than any other painter, opened himself to the impression which the outside world – that is, his subject – made on his eyes. He was driven by an indefatigable, almost insatiable, urge to paint. In 1885 he wrote from Etretat: . . . *to reproduce everything one needs two hands and hundreds of canvases.*[79] Perhaps it would have needed not just two, but hundreds of hands to capture that 'momentariness' which continually changes, slips past and re-emerges. His obstinate attempts to attain the unattainable are to his credit, but on the whole his serial pictures are a failure – even though on the highest and most highly respected level.

In the spring of 1889 near Fresselines, at the confluence of the Petite Creuse and the Grande Creuse, Monet painted the first pictures which, taken together, should be considered as a series in the sense of the aesthetic he was to establish in the second half of his career. He painted eight horizontal and two square pictures of roughly the same scene – the course of the Creuse as it flows through a gorge and vanishes into the distance. While the various versions hardly differ from each other in composition, they do so in their colours and in their treatment of light and shade. They were painted at different times of day and portray the spectrum of the effect of light and colour on a particular motif according to the position of the sun and the prevailing weather conditions. The scene looks like a single stage set with different lighting effects. Monet uses subtle shading and combinations of colours, either touching or in contrast with one another.

How hard he struggled to create this first, unified example of serial painting is clear from his letters. On 24 April he wrote to Alice in despair from Fresselines: . . . *The weather is terrible again. It's raining cats and dogs, so I'm staying in my room. I've no wish, in my present state, to become seriously indisposed, but that doesn't prevent me from worrying, because, if this keeps up, all my pictures will be ruined. I have four or five possible ones at the moment. I've never had such bad luck, because from the very start, as soon as I had some pictures that were going well, the weather broke and I had to make alterations within a few days because everything had changed – during these last few days as well, because everything's growing terribly fast . . .*

If *everything is growing terribly fast*, it must have meant that the colours which Monet had already applied had changed, compelling him in his dedication to natural verisimilitude to modify the canvases he had begun and then laid aside, so that the work he had already done must have been in vain. After a long forced break he finally went to work again and reported to Alice on 5 May: *What joy it gave me to see the wonderful weather, but what a disappointment when I got to a place I'd been unable to visit for three weeks. So many changes, and the sun reflected in the water like sparkling diamonds. I almost gave up, it was so dazzling, but it hurts to abandon a whole series and, believe me, I got used to it. And if I have another three or four days like this, I'll be saved.*[80]

From 1896 Monet embarked on a second large series of river paintings, only finishing it two years later with the 22nd picture: *Morning on the Seine* or *Arm of the Seine near Giverny*. Here he had found a composition which well suited his feeling for atmospheric colouring. Reflected in the expanses of water which take up the lower half of most of these horizontal canvases are groups of trees and bushes covering the banks almost like virgin growth. There is only a small piece of sky at the top right; the rest is filled with a hazy mass of leafy branches and treetops. In the whole series Monet restricted himself to subtle, related colours spread decoratively over the canvas in a variety of shades and in vague formations. The actual world of riverside greenery seems to melt into the simulated world of its reflections in the water and often the division between the two is scarcely discernible; the transitions seem fluid, smoothed out. Everything appears to be woven into a harmony of colour and form, in which the delicate, often mistily veiled, nuances of colour convey the painter's impression of mood at a specific time of day (mostly the morning). Only a few but crucial recurring motifs – such as the hazy line of the horizon or the treetops rising in silhouette in front of the pale sky –prevent these pictures from being meaningless. Monet is luxuriating in the ultimate in abstract colour formations, which were to find their climax in the later water lily paintings.

Some three to four years after painting some landscapes with small haystacks near his home in 1884/85, Monet began on a systematic series of 25 pictures of larger stacks. The whole cycle is divided into several smaller sub-groups with differing compositions. *At the start, I was just like everyone else. I thought two canvases would be enough, one for cloudy weather and one for sunshine. But no sooner had I begun to paint the sunshine than the lighting changed, so that two canvases were no longer enough if I was to render a truthful impression of a specific aspect of nature and not end up with a picture compiled from a number of different impressions.*[81] The ever-recurring lapidary, almost banal, subject appears in many different kinds of light, not only depending on the time of day but also on the season, and in each case the appeal of its colouring is sensitively determined. With his experience of painting winter landscapes, Monet also endeavoured to give his snow, which is never pure white, every possible variation of shade, colour and reflected light.

The great success of this series when it was put on show horrified Pissarro – once Monet's fellow-activist – who wrote, baffled, to his son Lucien on 3 April 1891: 'But for the moment people are only asking for Monets; it seems that he doesn't produce enough. The worst thing is that everyone wants to have *Haystacks at sunset!!!*... Always the same routine. Everything he produces leaves for America, fetching four, five or six thousand francs.'[82] On 9 April he added in a further letter to his son ' . . . He [de Bellio] has informed me that Monet is going to have a solo exhibition at Durand-Ruel's, of *nothing but haystacks.* The dealers Boussod et Valadon have told me that all the enthusiasts are only demanding haystacks. I can't imagine how annoying it must be for Monet to be confined to repeating himself – that is the terrible result of success!'[83] Leaving on one side the patent envy in these remarks from an Impressionist colleague, even like-minded painters of the time clearly found Monet's move into serial pictures difficult or even impossible to comprehend. Although Pissarro – certainly wrongly! – purported to detect in the repetition of the same motif a desire to satisfy market demands, the fact of his criticism shows another point of view, which to this day basically justifies objections to Monet's series: the convenience of repeating in a number of works a single composition and hence only having to spend the time and effort to work out form and style once for each series, in order to devote oneself exclusively to variations in colour and atmosphere. Since the routine of 'repetition' was almost bound to open the door to superficiality and rhetorical decorativeness, therein does in fact lie a weakness in Monet's concept of serial painting.

'Haystack near Giverny,' 1886. Schtschukin Collection,
Hermitage, St Petersburg

Another objection concerns the single pictures within such a series. On various occasions Monet stated that only as a whole could his series achieve their effect and be convincing. Also in his latter years he exhibited his series more or less in their entirety. However, when he allowed pictures from them to be sold singly, thereby dismembering the series, he was basically betraying his concept and his conviction. Today almost all the series have been scattered to the four winds and in a few museums – for instance, the Musée d'Orsay in Paris – one can only find fragments of them. The 'holistic impression' which was so important to Monet can only be fully experienced in books such as catalogues – an inadequate substitute! As Monet frequently modified in his studio the colours of serial pictures he had painted out-of-doors, thereby partially robbing them of their plein-air originality, he was being unfaithful to the natural authenticity to which he had paid lip-service all his life. In his later years solid objects in his pictures became anything but unimportant or interchangeable – in no way just formal means to a decorative, colourful end.

In 1891 and 1892 he produced a series of 23 pictures of a row of poplars by the Epte, a tributary of the Seine about two kilometres from his house. With few exceptions he fundamentally used one and the same composition, with the vertical row of poplar trunks and foliage in the foreground and behind this latticework the poplars seen from behind as they continue diagonally into the distance along a curve of the stream. The zigzag line of the treetops form a skilful counterbalance to the vertical trunks and the horizontal riverbank in the foreground. This linear composition – unusual for Monet – lends this series an almost constructivist character.

Noticeable, and possibly as a conscious corrective to this kind of draughtsmanship, is the emphatically artistic format which differs from picture to picture and consists of either heavily applied, patchy or delicate single spots of paint. On the whole the technical execution of these poplar pictures is freer and more spontaneous than that of other series. Here Monet plays on a rich scale of related shades of colour and complementary contrasts. In some of these paintings the weather is misty or dull as often as it is sunny with white clouds in the blue sky or the intense yellow-gold glitter of sunlit trees against the serene celestial blue. Here, too, the sophisticated composition of the pictures is undoubtedly modelled on coloured Japanese woodcuts.

Astonishingly, the three most famous Impressionist landscape painters – Monet, Pissarro and Sisley – all devoted themselves not only to reproducing the natural world but frequently also the man-made environment, with a preference for buildings. In his single pictures from the first half of his career Monet was already painting individual buildings or complete architectural ensembles at relatively regular intervals and obviously with great affection.

In 1892 and 1893 he concentrated on painting the gothic cathedral of Rouen or, more precisely, a part of its main façade. Because the painter needed to move his position while working, the 28 pictures in the series can be divided into groups, according to the different sections of the subject they portray. Whether or not the towers are included differs from picture to picture but some central elements are to be found in all of them: the three doorways with the rose window above and the vertical delineation of the pillars and the narrow strips of stone on the walls. Unlike in his earlier architectural paintings, Monet here breaks down the actually strongly coloured sections of the solid and clearly defined building by using amorphous materials. A subject which would normally lend itself more to being drawn in lines and contours is here treated purely from the viewpoint of the paint. As he spent over two years trying to evoke a momentary impression of this façade in different lights, according to the times of day, the seasons of the year and the weather, the architecture itself became his pretext, his medium and his aim.

'Rouen Cathedral in the afternoon sun,' 1892. Musée Marmottan, Paris

'Rouen Cathedral in the evening,' 1894. Pushkin Museum, Moscow

This aim was if possible to capture all the different combinations of light, shade and colour in which the surface of the cathedral façade variously appeared, in its plastic, spatial and atmospheric form. Like a relief map, a differently, artistically coloured structure greets us as we move from picture to picture. Together with the later water lily serial pictures, the cathedral series became the most famous ensemble of the second half of his career. While fulfilling the main principle of Impressionism (to fix the momentary appearance of a subject), it goes far beyond it: colour formations turn into a self-sufficient, decorative, abstracted pattern intended to make direct sensory contact with our eyes.

Starting in 1899, Monet carried this principle further with some more series based on architecture. From his London hotel window he painted two different views of the Thames, with the riverside buildings and the bridges as their formal components. The first series, of Charing Cross Bridge (now Hungerford Bridge), consisting entirely of vertical and horizontal lines, mostly parallel with the outlines of the canvas, creates a simpler constructional pattern than the second series – a diagonal view of Waterloo Bridge with its rounded arches. A third series draws one's eye to the Houses of Parliament from the opposite bank. The vertical lines of towers and buildings are contrasted with the horizontal line of the river, which is more 'sensed' than seen, as it is swathed in thick fog. All these views of the Thames are covered in a coloured veil to indicate the mist which sucks up all the details. Later Monet said to René Gimpel: *I only love London in winter . . . without its fog, London would not be a beautiful city. It is fog which gives it its wonderful breadth. Its massive, regular blocks become grandiose in this mysterious cloak.*[84] On the one hand the London fog inspired him because it had the effect of 'artistically' softening hard contours, but on the other the diffused light and subtle changes in the weather brought the sensitive painter to the brink of despair. His letters make clear the struggle he had with his London subjects, as for instance when he wrote to his wife Alice on 22 February 1901: *After getting up at 5.30 I thought I was in for a fine day, but no such luck! The fog has returned and I've remained at my post, steadfastly hoping that it might clear and not daring to start writing this. It changed the whole day long. I picked up first one canvas and then another, only to have to lay them aside a moment later. I was nearly distracted in the end, not knowing what I have been doing. Even this evening at the hospital {from which he was painting the Houses of Parliament} the weather wasn't good. I really have had a run of bad luck. Yesterday I'd barely settled down when it started to snow so heavily that I was covered all over and couldn't see a thing, it was coming down so hard. We've now had almost a week without sun, and I'm sure that I won't be able to make good progress with my canvases, even when it returns. It's madding, yet I feel I'm on the road to better things. In any case, I won't lose heart – quite the contrary.*[85] The difficulties caused by the weather compelled him – now in his 60s – to bring the whole series home and complete it over the next three years in his studio, rather than directly in front of his subject, no doubt mainly in order to vary the colouring in each picture . . . *because the impression created by the complete series is far more important.*[86]

The 95 pictures which make up the series of scenes of the Thames fall into three groups: 35 of Charing Cross Bridge, 41 of Waterloo Bridge and 19 of the Houses of Parliament. Taken as a whole, these pictures differ widely in colour, chiaroscuro contrasts and brushwork. They range from the subtlest, misty paints to vigorous, thickly applied brushstrokes revealing an expressive quality rare in Monet's work. Not only in subject but also in colouring, form and rendition of shimmering light, these London views are strongly reminiscent of the paintings by Turner which Monet probably saw and studied again during his stay in London at the turn of the century.

'Parliament, London.
Stormy sky,' 1904.
Musée des Beaux-Arts,
Lille

The same applies to the series of scenery and buildings painted in Venice in 1908. Here, too, Turner, who had a great love of Venice, was his model, both in subject matter and form, though in contrast to him, Monet was following his principle of serial painting. In all he created eight smaller series of 34 pictures. Not hackneyed views of the Doge's Palace or the Church of the Salute, but the façades of private palaces were his most rewarding subjects. Rather than choosing popular tourist treatment of his themes, he followed the Japanese style of presenting them in unusual ways. The lower half of eight of these pictures consists of water with reflections, while the upper half comprises buildings cut off by the edge of the canvas and in six cases a fragment of sky, though there is none in the wide painting of the Palazzo da Mula. These are studies of the harmony between the walls of the houses and the water, between hard and soft, tangible and amorphous. The atmospheric glitter of the water is superbly captured, as is the sequence of contrasts between dark windows and doorways and light-coloured walls, the whole swimming together in its reflections in the water. Monet had embraced the most intimate and charming aspect of Venice in an incomparable manner.

After painting, landscaping the garden at Giverny became Monet's second great passion. The two went together, for as his grounds grew in artistic charm they provided him with the principal and also the most important subjects for his pictures in the last decades of his life, now that he was less and less undertaking tiring journeys. His garden motifs appear almost exclusively in series; single pictures hardly feature any more. Only having to walk a short way to his subject, being able to work undisturbed on his own property and having real natural scenery (created by himself) ready to hand for painting, pointed and prepared the way towards serial painting. His pictures of his

'Palazzo Dario, Venice,' 1908. The Art Institute of Chicago

grounds, which he beautified and enlarged by purchasing more land, fall into two main iconographic groups: the flower garden close to the house and the equally large water garden, lying on the other side of the railway line which cut through the property.

'Water lilies,'
1900. Mahmoud
Khalil Museum,
Cairo

The central feature of the water garden was the water-lily pond, bordered with weeping willows and other trees and shrubs and spanned at its narrowest point by a curving Japanese bridge. From 1897 Monet worked increasingly intensively in this terrain as both gardener and painter. A set of eight single pictures of water lilies were the precursors of his much more numerous series. These pictures are of water lilies in flower, singly or in small clusters, with leaves floating among them on the surface of the water. All these single pictures comprise simply the surface of the water, seen at an angle from above – no horizon, no background, no sky. Monet has achieved the effect of a patterned carpet, which in his subsequent water-lily pictures he elaborated further. In one of the 1900 series, consisting of 16 pictures, the Japanese bridge is the focal point of the composition. Between 1903 and 1908 he produced an intermediate series of 78 pictures, in which the actual water lilies and the pond are artistically woven together, with trees and sky only seen as reflections in the water. Between 1913 and 1926 came 120 works forming the final water-lily series, which reached its climax in the large-scale decorative canvases.

Looking back on his water lilies, Monet said in an interview with the art historian Marc Elder, published in 1924: *I had planted them purely for pleasure; I grew them with no thought of painting them. A landscape takes more than a day to get under your skin. And then, all at once, I had the revelation – how wonderful my pond was – and reached for my palette. I've had hardly any other subject since that moment.*[87] The choice of such a subject corresponded to the zeitgeist: many art nouveau pictures and decorations feature ornamental flowers, including lilies. Monet's preference for his water-lily pond may have had to do with Turner's paintings of light and reflections in water. The main interest of the younger man was undoubtedly to decorate his canvases with the differing appearances and combinations of colours which could be created by the effect of light. This is like composing music – but with colours instead of sounds. The actual objects in the pictures seemed to become more and more irrelevant; people have often related Monet's strongly abstracted water-lily pictures to the current rise of abstract painting itself. However similar they may outwardly seem, 'abstracted' and 'abstract' are worlds apart. Monet never crossed the boundary into non-representational painting, for good reasons because, however transcendental and decorative his later serial pictures may be, in them – as in his whole œuvre – Monet's starting point was what he saw, what was visible. In spite of all simplification and blurring, the portrayal stems from the object to give even these pictures an inner meaning. An ever enhanced degree of draughtsmanship in the representation of objects can be discerned in the great murals which he presented to the French State and which, in spite of all the artistic delicacy of their monumental craftsmanship, are also somewhat forbidding.

On the other hand some of the other paintings of his gardens show Monet as fresher and less jaded. In 1900 he began on two single pictures and two small series, of his orchard and flower garden respectively. In 1912, and again between 1922 and 1924, his house appears behind thickly and exuberantly painted flowering shrubs and trees. Perhaps because, or even although, his sight had deteriorated around this time both before and after his eye operations, he achieved some thrilling work with unprecedentedly strong colouring and uninhibited shapes, which left far behind the fauves and expressionists who by then had again become tame.

Other subjects from his garden appear in the unparalleled, vital, artistic ebullience of an old man, such as Japanese-style snaking stems of lilies on the edge of the pond. In 1919 he also started painting the trees in his garden, for instance a weeping willow in strong impasto and brightly glittering but not garish colours. He

'The Japanese Bridge,' 1918 – 1924. Musée Marmottan, Paris

also returned to the Japanese bridge in a larger series of horizontal pictures. With passionate thrusts of his brush he created ghostly colour formations, which from a distance evoke a memory of the original motif. These are ecstasies, fantasies, symphonies in colour. It does not matter whether or not future generations attribute this later exuberance mainly to Monet's failing sight: in these works the master of Giverny became an Expressionist. This is the culmination of an artistic journey from Impression to Expression.

It is not the charmingly decorative water-lily pictures (greatly over-estimated today) and not at all the serial pictures of the second half of his career which determine Claude Monet's true greatness and importance, but much more the outstanding single paintings of his first, Impressionist period, which in their individual orthography and originality cannot be surpassed by the later serial output. To them should be added the utterly spontaneous, undisciplined, fascinatingly strongly expressive garden pictures from his last decade, on which an irresponsible old man was employing all the elements of 20th-century painting. Those who came after him only offered single aspects, such as action-painting, tachism or abstract expressionism from the New Fauves[88] and others. Monet, in his unsurpassed feeling for the splendour of colour, led the way from realism through Impressionism into an autonomous world of expression through colour, which is valid to this day.

NOTES

The whereabouts of the more important paintings mentioned in the text are (so far as is known) given on first mention in brackets. 'Paris' mostly means the Musée d'Orsay, less often the Musée Marmottan, in which a large part of Monet's legacy is to be found. The works quoted here are given in abbreviated form. The full titles are to be found in the Bibliography.

1. Wildenstein, p 23
2. E.g. Stuckey: *Monet* and Wildenstein: *Monet.* In his catalogue Wildenstein gives largely whole-page illustrations of the serial paintings, while reproducing the works from the first half of the painter's career in tiny format and thereby making a subjective judgment.
3. In the new edition of his catalogue (Wildenstein: *Monet*) the author has unfortunately not given the German version of the letters which he gave in the French original in the first edition.
4. On the history of Impressionism see particularly Rewald: *History of Impressionism*; Bellony-Rewald: *The lost World of the Impressionists*; Feist: *Impressionism*; Rewald: *From Van Gogh to Gauguin*;
5. Stuckey, p 204
6. Stuckey, p 205
7. Stuckey, p 271
8. Wildenstein, *Monet* vol 1, p18
9. Wildenstein, vol 1, p 18
10. Stuckey, *Monet* p 206
11. Stuckey, p 206
12. Stuckey, p 206/7
13. Stuckey, p 271
14. Stuckey, p 207
15. Stuckey, p 217

16. Rewald, *History* p 47
17. Wildenstein, vol 1, p 40
18. Stuckey, p 207
19. Stuckey, p 207f
20. Stuckey, p 272/3
21. Stuckey, p 273
22. for the Salon exhibitions, see Rewald, p 46ff
23. Küster, p 16
24. Küster, p 16
25. Sagner-Düchting, Karin, *Claude Monet,* p 23
26. Küster, p 21
27. Küster, p 21
28. Küster, p 22
29. Wildenstein, vol 1, p 69
30. Poulain, Gaston *Bazille et ses amis* p 119
31. Wildenstein, vol 1, p 74
32. Poulain, p 224
33. Küster, p 28
34. Wildenstein, vol 1, p 78
35. Küster, p 28
36. Wildenstein, vol 1, p 84
37. Stuckey, p 218
38. Sagner-Düchting, p 49
39. Wildenstein, vol 1, p 86
40. Stuckey, p 273
41. Stuckey, p 266
42. Dewhurst, William, *Impressionist Painting* p 217
43. Küster, p 33
44. Küster, p 34
45. Wildenstein, p 94
46. See Rewald, *History* p 189ff
47. Küster, p 50
48. Küster, p 48
49. Küster, p 49
50. (both) Küster p 52
51. Clemenceau, *Claude Monet* p 22.
52. Küster, p 56
53. Wildenstein, vol 1, p 147
54. Venturi, Lionello, *Les Archives de l'Impressionisme* vol 1, p 268

55. Wildenstein, vol 1, p 195

56. Küster, p 72

57. Leeuw, Ronald de, *The Letters of Vincent van Gogh* p359

58. See Stuckey, p 61

59. see Arnold, *Van Gogh,* 1995, p 615ff

60. Geffroy, Gustave, *Claude Monet*

61. Mallarmé, *Correspondance,* vol 3 (Gallimard, Paris) p 212

62. Stuckey, p 276

63. See Arnold, *Van Gogh* 1993, p 290ff; 1995 p 99; 1997, p 167ff

64. Wildenstein, vol 1, p 208

65. Stuckey, p 241

66. Küster, p 122

67. Koja, *Claude Monet,* p 88

68. see Busch: *Monet*

69. de Leeuw, p 422

70. Wildenstein, vol. 2, p 30

71. see Arnold, *Van Gogh* 1997, p 175ff

72. see Arnold, *Van Gogh,* 1997 p 176ff

73. Koja, p 100

74. Koja, p 102

75. Pissarro, *Letters to his son Lucien*, ed John Rewald, p 148.

76. Sagner-Düchting, p 148

77. Koja, p 104

78. Gasquet, Joachim, Cézanne, What he said to me, in *L'Amour de l'Art* (Paris: 1921)

79. Küster, p 73

80. Koja, p 112

81. Sagner-Düchting, p 158

82. Pissarro, p 229

83. Pissarro, p 231

84. Sagner-Düchting, p 178

85. Koja, p 130

86. Koja, p 131

87. Koja, p 146

88. 'Neue Wilden': a group, characterised by huge scale and raw energy, including Georg Baselitz and Anselm Kiefer, which flourished in Germany in the 1980s. Their open brushwork and gestures can be said to trace an aesthetic lineage back to Monet.

Chronology

Year	Age	Life
1840		Oscar-Claude Monet born in Paris, the second son of the businessman Claude-Adolphe Monet and his wife Louise-Justine, née Aubré.
1845	5	The family moved to Le Havre, where his father took a post in the firm of his brother-in-law, Jacques Lecadre. In the following year Oscar-Claude attended a private primary school and subsequently the town high school.
1856	16	In addition attended the town art school and started drawing caricatures for money.
1857	17	On 28 January his mother died. Eugène Boudin, marine painter, introduced him to painting.
1858	18	After the death of Jacques Lecadre his art-loving widow took an interest in her talented nephew.
1859	19	First period as a student in Paris, attending the Académie Suisse, where he met Camille Pissarro.
1861	21	In the summer started his military service in Algeria.

Year	History	Culture
1840	In New Zealand, Treaty of Waitangi: Maori chiefs surrender sovereignty to Britain. In Canada, Act of Union joins Lower and Upper Canada	R. Schumann, *Dichterliebe*. Adolphe Sax invents the saxophone. P J Proudhon, *Qu'est-ce-que la Propriété?*
1845	In Ireland, potato famine. In India, Anglo-Sikh War (until 1848-9).	Wagner, *Tannhäuser*. Friedrich Engels, *The Condition of the Working Classes in England*.
1856	In India, Britain annexes Oudh. Treaty of Paris: integrity of Turkey is recognised. Henry Bessemer discovers process of converting iron into steel.	Liszt, *Hungarian Rhapsodies*. Karl Bechstein founds his piano factory. Robert Schumann dies. Ingres, *La Source*. Flaubert, *Madame Bovary*.
1857	In India, mutiny against the British (until 1858). In Africa, J H Speke 'discovers' source of the Nile. Laying of cable under Atlantic Ocean begun (until 1865).	Charles Baudelaire, *Les Fleurs du Mal*. Gustave Flaubert, *Madame Bovary*.
1858	Dissolution of English East India Company. At Lourdes, apparition of Virgin Mary.	Jacques Offenbach, *Orpheus in the Underworld*.
1859	Franco-Piedmontese War against Austria. Spanish-Moroccan War (until 1860). Construction of Suez Canal begins (until 1869).	C F Gounod, *Faust*. Wagner, *Tristan und Isolde*. George Eliot, *Adam Bede*. Edouard Manet, *Absinthe Drinker*.
1861	In US, Abraham Lincoln becomes president (until 1865); Civil War begins (until 1865). In France, Louis Pasteur develops germ theory of disease.	Dickens, *Great Expectations*. In Britain, William Morris begins to make wallpapers and tapestries.

Year	Age	Life
1862	22	After a serious illness in the summer spent six months' convalescent leave at home. His aunt Lecadre bought him out from military service. Resumed painting with Boudin and also with Johan Barthold Jongkind on the Normandy coast. In November returned to Paris, where he briefly attended the studio of the academic painter Charles Gleyre, where he became friends with Alfred Sisley, Auguste Renoir and Frédéric Bazille, who was well-off. As his father and aunt subsequently refused to support him, he turned repeatedly to Bazille for help.
1863	23	Painted with his friends at Chailly in the Forest of Fontainebleau.
1864	24	Spent Easter at Chailly and then worked with Bazille near Honfleur. Participated in an exhibition in Rouen and sold his first pictures (to the ship-owner Gaudibert).
1865	25	Joined Bazille in his Paris studio at 6 Rue de Furstemberg. Two seascapes accepted by the Salon. At Chailly began preparations for the large painting *Luncheon on the Grass*, which he later abandoned.
1866	26	Success at the Salon with *Camille or Woman in the Green Dress*. Camille Doncieux, his mistress, was also his model for *Women in the Garden*. To avoid his creditors, fled from Sèvres to the Normandy coast, where his family gave him board and lodging.
1867	27	With Renoir shared Bazille's new Paris studio in Rue Visconti. Rejected by the Salon. Bazille bought *Women in the Garden*. With Renoir painted views of Paris. On 8 August his first son Jean was born to Camille in Paris.
1868	28	One seascape accepted by the Salon. Stayed in Bennecourt on the Seine and on the Normandy coast. Exhibited five paintings in the International Seafaring Exhibition in Le Havre. Gaudibert supported him with purchases and commissions.
1869	29	Exhibited several times in the shop-window of the Paris paint-seller Latouche. In the summer went to Bougival on the Seine, living there in extreme poverty. Painted *La Grenouillère* with Renoir.

Year	History	Culture
1862	In Prussia, Otto von Bismarck becomes premier.	Verdi, *La Forza del Destino*. Hugo, *Les Misérables*.
1863	In US, slavery abolished. In Asia, Cambodia becomes French protectorate. Polish uprising against Russia.	Berlioz, *The Trojans* (part I). Manet, *Déjeuner sur l'herbe*.
1864	In London, Karl Marx organizes first socialist international. British, French and Dutch fleets attack Japanese in Shimonoseki Straits. Henri Dunant founds Red Cross. Louis Pasteur invents pasteurisation.	Anton Bruckner, *Mass No 1 in D minor*. Leo Tolstoy, *War and Peace* (until 1869).
1865	In US, Abraham Lincoln assassinated. End of transport of convicts to Australia.	Lewis Carroll, *Alice's Adventures in Wonderland*.
1866	Austro-Prussian War. Austro-Italian War. Alfred Nobel invents dynamite. Gregor Mendel develops laws of heredity.	Friedrich Smetana, *The Bartered Bride*. Fyodor Dostoevsky, *Crime and Punishment*.
1867	Prussia forms North German Confederation. Austria forms Austro-Hungarian empire. Joseph Lister introduces antiseptic surgery.	Giuseppe Verdi, *Don Carlos*. Johann Strauss, *The Blue Danube*. Marx, *Das Kapital*. Henrik Ibsen, *Peer Gynt*.
1868	In Britain, William Gladstone becomes prime minister (until 1874). In Japan, Meiji dynasty restored. In Britain, Trades' Union Congress founded.	Johannes Brahms, *A German Requiem*. Dostoevsky, *The Idiot*.
1869	Suez Canal opens.	R. Wagner, *The Rhinegold*.

Year	Age	Life
1870	30	On 28 June married Camille in Paris. Later went to Trouville, where he painted beach scenes with Boudin. On 7 July his aunt Lecadre died. Because of the Franco-Prussian War fled with his family to London, where he met Daubigny and Pissarro. Taken on by he art-dealer Durand-Ruel. Bazille killed in action on 28 November.
1871	31	On 17 January his father died at Le Havre. With Pissarro studied Turner's and Constable's paintings in the London museums. In the summer painted at Zaandamm in Holland, in the autumn again in Paris. In December rented a house at Argenteuil on the Seine.
1872	32	Began painting river scenes at Argenteuil, sometimes from his newly acquired houseboat. In Le Havre painted *Impression, sunrise.*
1873	33	At Argenteuil met the wealthy painter Gustave Caillebotte. Preparations for a group exhibition.
1874	34	Early in the year in Holland. From 15 April to 15 May first Impressionist exhibition in the Boulevard des Capucines in Paris overwhelmingly rejected by the press. *Impression, sunrise* gave rise to the derisory term 'impressionist', which later gained acceptance as the serious name for this style. In the summer moved to another house in Argenteuil, where Manet and Renoir visited him.
1875	35	Financial situation once more deteriorated. Disappointing returns from the auction of Impressionist pictures in the Hotel Drouot in Paris.
1876	36	Met the collector Victor Choquet. Caillebotte began to buy his pictures. On the invitation of the Parisian shop-owner and art speculator Ernest Hoschedé and his wife Alice, Monet painted large decorative panels for the dining-room in her country house at Rottembourg (among them the *Turkeys*). Camille seriously ill. Paintings of the Gare Saint-Lazare.
1877	37	Third Impressionist exhibition in April.

Year	History	Culture
1870	Franco-Prussian War. Papal Rome annexed by Italy. In US, John Rockefeller founds Standard Oil.	Clément Delibes, *Coppélia*. Dostoevsky, *The House of the Dead*.
1871	At Versailles, William I proclaimed German emperor. In France, Third Republic suppresses Paris Commune and loses Alsace-Lorraine to Germany. In Africa, H M Stanley finds D Livingston at Ujiji.	Stravinsky, *The Rite of Spring*. Guillaume Apollinaire, *Les peintres cubistes*. D H Lawrence, *Sons and Lovers*. Marcel Proust, *A la recherche du temps perdu* (until 1927).
1872	In Philippines, rebellion against Spain.	Thomas Hardy, *Under the Greenwood Tree*.
1873	In Spain, Amadeo I abdicates; republic proclaimed. Great Depression (until 1896).	Arthur Rimbaud, *A Season in Hell*. Walter Pater, *Studies in the History of the Renaissance*.
1874	In Britain, Benjamin Disraeli becomes prime minister. In Spain, Alfonso XII establishes constitutional monarchy.	Smetana, *My Fatherland*. J Strauss, *Die Fledermaus*.
1875	In Bosnia and Herzegovina, revolts against Turkish rule. Alexander Graham Bell patents telephone.	Tchaikovsky, *First Piano Concerto in B-flat minor*. Georges Bizet, *Carmen*. Mark Twain, *The Adventures of Tom Sawyer* (until 1876).
1876	In US, Battle of Little Bighorn; General Custer dies.	Johannes Brahms, *First Symphony*. Wagner, *Siegfried*; first complete performance of Wagner's *The Ring*.
1877	Queen Victoria proclaimed empress of India. Russo-Turkish War. Thomas Edison invents gramophone.	Emile Zola, *L'Assommoir*.

Year	Age	Life
1878	38	On 17 March his second son Michel born. Hoschedé declared bankrupt in the spring and his collection auctioned in the summer, with low prices paid for Monet's pictures. Still. In August moved to Vétheuil on the Seine, where the impoverished Hoschedés and their children followed them. Worsening state of Camille's health.
1879	39	Fourth Impressionist exhibition in Paris. On 5 September.Camille died at Vétheuil.
1880	40	Again represented in the Salon. Exhibition of his work in the Paris premises of the magazine *La Vie Moderne*. Painted *Blocks of Ice at Vétheuil*.
1881	41	In spring and summer worked on the Normandy coast. In December moved to Poissy on the Seine, where Alice Hoschedé followed him against her husband's wishes.
1882	42	Took part in the seventh Impressionist exhibition in Paris. Worked in Dieppe and Pourville.
1883	43	In January at Etretat. From 28 February first solo exhibition at Durand-Ruel's in Paris. On 3 May Manet's funeral. In April/May moved to Giverny near Vernon on the Seine. Painted decorations for Durand'Ruel's private house. At the end of the year visited Cézanne in L'Estaque in company with Renoir and travelled briefly as far as Genoa.
1884	44	Returned to the Mediterranean in the middle of January for three months, painting mainly in Bordighera.
1885	45	From 15 May participation in an exhibition in Georges Petit's gallery in Paris. In the autumn stayed in Etretat for three months with his family.
1886	46	From 6 February participated in the exhibition of the 'Twenty' in Brussels. From April successful Impressionist exhibition in New York (49 works of his included). End of April short journey to Holland. From 15 May eighth and last Impressionist exhibition in Paris, in which he did not participate. From September stayed on Belle-Ile in Brittany, where he met Gustave Geffroy, who became his first biographer.

Year	History	Culture
1878	Congress of Berlin resolves Balkan crisis. Serbia becomes independent. Britain gains Cyprus. In London, electric street lighting.	Tchaikovsky, *Swan Lake*.
1879	In Africa, Zulu War. In south Africa, Boers proclaim Transvaal Republic.	Anton Bruckner, *Sixth Symphony*. Tchaikovsky, *Eugene Onegin*. Ibsen, *The Doll's House*. August Strindberg, *The Red Room*.
1880	In Britain, William Gladstone becomes prime minister. First Boer War (until 1881). Louis Pasteur discovers streptococcus.	Tchaikovsky, *1812 Overture*. Dostoevsky, *The Brothers Karamazov*.
1881	Tunisia becomes French protectorate. In Algeria, revolt against the French. In eastern Europe, Jewish pogroms.	Jacques Offenbach, *The Tales of Hoffmann*. Henry James, *Portrait of Lady*. Ibsen, *Ghosts*.
1882	Fenians murder Lord Cavendish in Phoenix Park, Dublin.	A. Dvorak, *Dimitrij*.
1883	Jewish immigration to Palestine (Rothschild Colonies). Germany acquires southwest Africa. In Chicago, world's first skyscraper built.	Antonín Dvorák, *Stabat Mater*. Robert Louis Stevenson, *Treasure Island*.
1884	Sino-French War (until 1885). Berlin Conference to mediate European claims in Africa (until 1885).	Mark Twain, *Huckleberry Finn*. Georges Seurat, *Une Baignade, Asnières*.
1885	Belgium's King Leopold II establishes Independent Congo State. In Transvaal, gold discovered. Gottlieb Daimler invents prototype of motorcycle.	Zola, *Germinal*. Guy de Maupassant, *Bel Ami*.
1886	In Cuba, slavery abolished. In India, first meeting of National Congress. In Canada, Canadian Pacific Railway completed.	Stevenson, *Dr Jekyll and Mr Hyde*. Rimbaud, *Les Illuminations*. Leo Tolstoy, *The Death of Ivan Ilich*.

Year	Age	Life
1887	47	Further successful participation in an exhibition at Georges Petit's; from 25 May participation in the second Impressionist exhibition at Durand-Ruel's gallery in New York.
1888	48	From January to April painted on the Côte d'Azur, from which ten pictures were exhibited in June at Boussod & Valadon (Goupil) in Paris through a contract with Théo van Gogh. Travelled to London in the summer. Refused the Legion of Honour. Began the series of *Haystacks*.
1889	49	In February 20 works exhibited at Goupil's in London. In the spring painted in the Creuse valley, where he produced his first serial paintings. Showed three pictures at the World Exhibition in Paris. In the summer a large retrospective (together with Auguste Rodin) at Petit's gallery. In the autumn raised money to purchase Manet's *Olympia*, which was eventually acquired by the state.
1890	50	Bought the house at Giverny. On 29 July Vincent van Gogh died.
1891	51	On 18 March Ernst Hoschedé died in Paris. In May the *Haystack* series was exhibited by Durand-Ruel. Started on the *Poplar* series. In December went to London
1892	52	From February worked on the *Rouen Cathedral* series. On 16 July married Alice Hoschedé.
1893	53	Continued the *Rouen Cathedral* series.
1894	54	Paul Cézanne visited Giverny.
1895	55	From the end of January spent two months in Norway. Spring exhibition by Durand-Ruel of the *Rouen Cathedral* series.
1896	56	In the spring again painted on the Normandy coast and began the series *Morning on the Seine*.

Year	History	Culture
1887	In Britain, Queen Victoria celebrates Golden Jubilee. Heinrich Hertz produces radio waves.	Verdi, *Otello*.
1888	In Germany, William II becomes emperor (until 1918). In Asia, French Indo-China established.	N Rimsky-Korsakov, *Scheherezade* (op 35). Rudyard Kipling, *Plain Tales from the Hills*. Strindberg, *Miss Julie*. George Eastman invents the first commercial roll-film camera: the 'Kodak' box.
1889	Second Socialist International. In Paris, Eiffel Tower completed.	Richard Strauss, *Don Juan*. Verdi, *Falstaff*. George Bernard Shaw, *Fabian Essays*.
1890	In Germany, Otto von Bismarck dismissed. In Spain, universal suffrage.	Tchaikovsky, *The Queen of Spades*. Paul Cézanne, *The Cardplayers*. Ibsen, *Hedda Gabler*.
1891	Building of Trans-Siberian railway begins.	Tchaikovsky, *The Nutcracker*. Oscar Wilde, *The Picture of Dorian Gray*. Henri Toulouse-Lautrec, *Le bal du Moulin-Rouge*. Paul Gaugin goes to Tahiti.
1892	In Britain, Gladstone becomes Prime Minister	Maurice Maeterlinck, *Pelleas et Mélisande*
1893	Franco-Russian alliance signed. France annexes Laos.	Dvorák, *From the New World*. Tchaikovsky, *Pathétique*. Wilde, *A Woman of No Importance*.
1894	In France, President Carnot assassinated. In France, Alfred Dreyfus convicted of treason.	Claude Debussy, *L'Après-midi d'un Faune*. Kipling, *The Jungle Book*. G B Shaw, *Arms and Man*.
1895	Lumière brothers invent the cinematograph. Guglielmo Marconi invents wireless telegraphy. Wilhelm Röntgen invents X-rays.	H G Wells, *The Time Machine*. W B Yeats, *Poems*. Wilde, *The Importance of Being Earnest*.
1896	First Olympic Games of the modern era held in Athens. Antoine (Henri) Becquerel discovers radioactivity of uranium.	Giacomo Puccini, *La Bohème*. Thomas Hardy, *Jude the Obscure*.

Year	Age	Life
1897	57	From January back in Normandy. Built the second studio at Giverny. His son Jean married his stepsister Blanche Hoschedé. First *Water lilies* series.
1898	58	In June large solo exhibition at Petit's gallery.
1899	59	Exhibitions in Paris and New York. In the autumn in London. Began the series of views of the Thames.
1900	60	In London again to continue the series. In the summer painted at Vétheuil. Solo exhibition at Durand-Ruel's. *Water lilies.*
1901	61	Again at Vétheuil and in London.
1902	62	In February exhibited at Bernheim-Jeune in Paris.
1903	63	Began completing the Thames views in Giverny. On 12 November Pissarro died. *Water lilies.*
1904	64	In May Durand-Ruel exhibited Thames views. In the autumn went to Spain with Alice.
1906	66	On 22 October Cézanne died.
1908	68	Troubles with his eyes. In the autumn went with Alice to Venice to paint. *Water lilies.*

Year	History	Culture
1897	In Britain, Queen Victoria celebrates Diamond Jubilee. J J Thomson discovers electron.	Joseph Conrad, *The Nigger of the Narcissus*. Stefan George, *Das Jahr der Seele*. Edmond Rostand, *Cyrano de Bergerac*.
1898	Spanish-American War: Spain loses Cuba, Puerto Rico and the Philippines. Britain conquers Sudan.	Henry James, *The Turn of the Screw*. H G Wells, *The War of the Worlds*. Zola, *J'Accuse*. Auguste Rodin, *The Kiss*.
1899	Second Boer War (until 1902).	Hector Berlioz, *The Taking of Troy*. Edward Elgar, *Enigma Variations*.
1900	First Pan-African Conference. In France, Dreyfus pardoned. In China, Boxer Rebellion (until 1901). Aspirin introduced. First Zeppelin flight.	Puccini, *Tosca*. Conrad, *Lord Jim*. Sigmund Freud, *The Interpretation of Dreams*.
1901	In Britain, Queen Victoria dies; Edward VII becomes king. In US, William McKinley assassinated; Theodore Roosevelt becomes president.	Strindberg, *The Dance of Death*. Kipling, *Kim*. Anton Chekhov, *The Three Sisters*. Pablo Picasso begins Blue Period (until 1904).
1902	Peace of Vereeniging ends Boer War. Anglo-Japanese alliance.	Debussy, *Pelléas et Mélisande*. Scott Joplin, *The Entertainer*. Arthur Conan Doyle, *The Hound of the Baskervilles*. Conrad, *The Heart of Darkness*. André Gide, *L'Immoraliste*.
1903	In Britain, suffragette movement begins. Panama Canal Zone granted to US to build and manage waterway.	Henry James, *The Ambassadors*.
1904	France and Britain sign Entente Cordiale. Photoelectric cell invented.	Puccini, *Madama Butterfly*. Jack London, *The Sea Wolf*. J M Barrie, *Peter Pan*. Chekhov, *The Cherry Orchard*.
1906	France and Germany over Morocco. Dreyfus rehabilitated.	Henri Matisse, *Bonheur de vivre*. Maxim Gorky, *The Mother*.
1908	Young Turks revolt in Resina. Crete proclaims union with Greece.	Gustav Mahler, *Das Lied von der Erde* (until 1909). E M Forster, *A Room with a View*. Cubism begins with Picasso and Braque.

Year	Age	Life
1911	71	On 19 May Alice died at Giverny. A personal and artistic crisis began.
1912	72	Cataract diagnosed in both eyes.
1914	74	On 10 February his elder son Jean died and his widow Blanche Hoschedé immediately took on the task of caring for him. Clemenceau encouraged him to paint large decorative panels of water lilies, for which he started building a third, more spacious studio at Giverny. His son Michel called up into the army.
1916	76	The new studio finished.
1917	77	In October travelled to Le Havre, Etretat and Honfleur.
1918	78	On the occasion of the Armistice Monet decided to donate some pictures to the state, which led to long drawn-out negotiations in the following years in which Clemenceau took part.
1919	79	On 17 December Renoir died.
1920	80	Decision to build a pavilion in the garden of the Hotel Biron in Paris to house his *Water lilies* series.
1921	81	The French state bought *Women in the Garden* for 200,000 francs and offered the Orangery at the Tuileries for the *Water lilies*.
1922	82	On 12 April, on Clemenceau's insistence, the contract of purchase was signed.
1923	83	In January and July respectively cataract operations on his eyes. In spite of his difficulties continued to work on his decorative paintings with the help of. coloured lenses.

Year	History	Culture
1911	Arrival of German gunboat in Agadir creates international crisis; Kaiser asserts Germany's 'Place in the Sun'. Roald Amundsen reaches South Pole.	R. Strauss, *Der Rosenkavalier*.
1912	Titanic sinks. Morocco becomes French protectorate. Dr Sun Yat-sen establishes Republic of China.	Arnold Schoenberg, *Pierrot lunaire*. Carl Jung, *The Psychology of the Unconscious*. Bertrand Russell, *The Problems of Philosophy*.
1914	28 June: Archduke Franz Ferdinand assassinated in Sarajevo. First World War begins. Panama Canal opens. Egypt becomes British protectorate.	James Joyce, *The Dubliners*. Ezra Pound, *Des Imagistes*.
1916	Battle of Somme. Battle of Jutland. Easter Rising in Ireland. Arabs revolt against Ottoman Turks.	Guillaume Apollinaire, *Le poète assassiné*. G B Shaw, *Pygmalion*. Dada movement launched in Zurich with Cabaret Voltaire.
1917	Pétain becomes French Commander-in-Chief; Pershing arrives in Paris to head US forces. October Revolution in Russia: Lenin becomes First Commissar. Allies execute Mata Hari.	First recording of New Orleans jazz. Franz Kafka, *Metamorphosis*. Giurgio de Chirico, *Le Grand Métaphysique*.
1918	Treaty of Brest-Litovsk. In Russia, murder of Imperial family	Plaul Klee, *Gartenplan*. Oswald Spengler, *The Decline of the West*.
1919	Treaty of Versaille	Colette, *Cherie*
1920	Foundation of League of Nations	Agatha Christie, *The Mysterious Affair at Styles*
1921	First meeting of League of Nations in Paris.	Edith Wharton, *The Age of Innocence*.
1922	Soviet Union formed. Benito Mussolini's fascists march on Rome.	T S Eliot, *The Waste Land*. Joyce, *Ulysses*.
1923	Ottoman empire ends; Palestine, Transjordan and Iraq to Britain; Syria to France	Le Corbusier, *Vers une architecture*.

Year	Age	Life
1924	84	Exhibitions in Paris and New York.
1925	86	*Water lilies* completed. In the summer an incurable lung disease diagnosed. On 5 December at the age of 86 he died in Clemenceau's presence at Giverny and was buried there.
1927		On 17 May the *Water lilies* panels were opened to the public in the Orangery.

Year	History	Culture
1924	Vladimir Lenin dies.	Forster, *A Passage to India*. Kafka, *The Hunger Artist*. Thomas Mann, *The Magic Mountain*. André Breton, first surrealist manifesto.
1925	Pact of Locarno. Chiang Kai-shek launches campaign to unify China. Discovery of ionosphere.	F Scott Fitzgerald, *The Great Gatsby*. Kafka, *The Trial*. Sergey Eisenstein, *Battleship Potemkin*. Television invented.
1927	Joseph Stalin comes to power. Charles Lindbergh flies across Atlantic.	Martin Heidegger, *Being and Time*. Virginia Woolf, *To the Lighthouse*.

Testimonials

Pissarro

Monet's talent is to my mind a very serious and a very pure one. His art is based on observation, and is utterly original in feeling – poetry produced by the harmony of true colours. A Bellony-Rewald, *The Lost World of the Impressionists*, p 119

Van Gogh (1888/89)

I prefer to wait for the generation to come, which will do for portraits what Claude Monet does for landscape – the rich, jaunty landscape à la Guy de Maupassant. (from Letter no 525 to Théo, Arles 15 August 1888)

Oh to paint figures like Claude Monet paints landscapes. In spite of everything that will still have to be done, and before among the impressionists one sees Monet alone. (from Letter no 590 to Théo, Arles 3 May 1889)

Émile Zola (1866)

I do not know Monet, nor do I think I have ever seen a single one of his pictures before. Yet I feel almost like an old friend of his, the reason being that, to me, his picture speaks whole volumes on the subject of strength and truth. Oh yes, here is someone with temperament – he is a man among all the eunuchs. Look at the pictures alongside: how pitiable they seem, compared to this window open on nature! Here we have more than a Realist:

someone who knows how to interpret every detail, carefully and powerfully, without becoming dull. (From 'Mon salon: Les réalistes au salon' in *L'Evènement,* Paris, 11 May 1866. Transl J Brownjohn (in Koja *Monet*)

Stéphane Mallarmé (1876)

Claude Monet loves water, and he has a special gift for portraying its movement and transparency, whether of sea or river, and whether uniformly grey or coloured by the sky. I have never yet seen a boat lying so naturally in the water as in his pictures or a veil lighter and more fluid than the breath of air which sets it in motion. It is truly a miracle.

Joris-Karl Huysmans (1883)

Monet, Pissarro and Sisley are the landscape painters for whom the term 'Impressionism' was coined. Monet has already been making splotches for some time, has ventured small improvisations, cobbled together little scraps of landscape, bitter salads of orange peel, green onions, and ribbons in a blue rinse which pretend they are the flowing water of a river. One thing is certain: this artist's vision was overwrought. But it is equally correct to say that his execution was sloppy – an obvious lack of practice. In spite of the talent shown in some of his sketches, I have to admit that I have gradually lost interest in his careless, hasty painting. Impressionism as Monet practised it led straight into a cul-de-sac. It was the permanently semi-hatched egg of realism – approaching reality, yet always abandoning it halfway through. It is undoubtedly Monet who has most contributed to convincing the public that the term 'Impressionism' simply describes a style of painting which never goes beyond confusing rudiments and vague, crude sketches.

Guy de Maupassant (1886)

I often followed Claude Monet when he was looking for new impressions. He reminded one less of a painter than of a hunter. A whole host of children followed him everywhere, carrying five or six canvases depicting the same motif at different times of day and with different effects. He took them up and laid them aside, according to the changes in weather and lighting. In front of his subject the painter lay in wait for sun and shade; with a few brushstrokes he captured a ray of light or a passing cloud... I saw him once catching a beam of shimmering light on a white cliff in a stream of shades of yellow, superbly reproducing the strikingly fleeting impression left behind by this hardly noticeable and yet dazzling reflection. Another time he took a shower of rain over the sea in his hands and splashed it against his canvas. And what he was painting like this was actual rain, which so darkened waves, cliffs and sun that one could not distinguish them any more in this deluge.

John Rewald (1946)

It may be doubted whether Monet really meant to 'discredit the object' [as Kandinsky suggested] in his attempt to observe methodically and with almost scientific exactness the uninter-rupted changes of light on various motifs . . . He became disgusted with 'easy things that come in a flash', although it had been precisely in those 'easy things' that he had manifested his genius for seizing in the first impression the luminous splendours of nature. The stubbornness with which he now pursued his race with light – he himself used the word 'stubbornness' in this connection – resulted in frequently brilliant solutions of the problem he tried to solve, but this problem itself remained close to being an experiment and imposed severe limitations. His eyes, straining to observe minute transformations, were apt to lose the perception of the whole. Thus Monet abandoned form completely (his pioneering in this field was to lead Kandinsky to totally new concepts) and sought to retain in a vibrant tissue of subtle nuances the single miracle of light.

Monet's series met with tremendous success . . . As to Monet's former comrades, they witnessed with a certain sadness how his career as an impressionist was ending in technical prowess. Admiring his talent and having tacitly considered him the leader of their group, they now remembered Degas' contention that Monet's art 'was that of a skilful but not profound decorator'.
The History of Impressionism, 4th revised edition 1973 pp 563/4

Further Reading

Arnold, Matthias. *Van Gogh* (Munich: 1993, 1995, 1997) No known English translation

Bellony-Rewald, Alice. *The Lost World of the Impressionists* (Weidenfeld & Nicholson, London: 1976)

Clemenceau, Georges. *Claude Monet, Cinquante ans d'amitié* (La Palatine, Paris, Geneva: 1965)

Dewhurst, William. *Impressionist Painting, its Genesis and Development* (London: 1904.)

Geffroy, Gustave. *Claude Monet, sa vie, son temps, son œuvre* (Paris: 1922)

Gwynn, S, *Claude Monet and his Garden* (London: 1934)

House, John, *Monet* (New York; Oxford: 1977)

Joyce, Claire, *Monet et Giverny* (London: 1975)

Koja, Stephan. *Claude Monet,* tr J Brownjohn (Prestel Verlag, Munich & New York: 1996)

Küster, Bernd, *Claude Monet, Ein Maler-Leben (The Life of an Artist)* (Hamburg: 1987) No known English translation

Leeuw, Ronald de (ed), *The Letters of Vincent Van Gogh* tr. Arnold Pomerans (Penguin, London: 1996)

Metropolitan Museum of Art Exhibition Catalogue, *Monet's Years at Giverny. Beyond Impressionism* (New York: 1978)

Petrie, Brian, *Claude Monet, the first of the Impressionists* (New York; Oxford: 1979)

Pissarro, Camille. *Letters to his son Lucien* ed John Rewald (Albin Michel, Paris: 1950)

Poulain, Gaston, *Bazille et ses amis* (Paris: 1932)

Rewald, John, *The History of Impressionism* (Metropolitan Museum of Art, New York: 1946; 4th revised edition 1973. Secker & Warburg, London: 1973)

Sagner-Düchting, Karin, *Claude Monet 1840-1926. A Feast for the Eyes* tr Karen

Williams (Taschen, Cologne: 1994)

Seiberling, Grace, *Monet's Series* (New York; London: 1981)

Stuckey, Charles F (ed.) *Claude Monet 1840-1926* 4 vols (Taschen, Cologne: 1994)

Tucker, Paul Hayes. *Monet at Argenteuil* (New Haven; London: 1982)

Venturi, Lionello. *Les Archives de l'impressionisme* (Burt Franklin, New York: 1968)

Wildenstein, Daniel, *Monet or the Triumph of Impressionism,* tr Chris Miller (Taschen, Cologne: 2003)

Wildenstein, Daniel, *Claude Monet,* in the series *The Impressionists* (Cassell, London: 1988)

Wildenstein, Daniel, *Claude Monet,* Biography and Catalogue Raisonnée, 4 vols (Lausanne, Paris: 1974-1991)

Picture Sources

The author and publishers wish to express their thanks to the following sources of illustrative material and/or permission to reproduce it. They will make the proper acknowdgements in future editions in the event that any ommissions have occurred.

Akg Images: pp. 11, 25, 26, 45, 69, 76/77, 84/85, 88/89, 90, 92/93, 98/99, 100/101, 108/109, 110, 112/113, 134/135, 138, 139, 142/143, 145,146/147, 148/149; Daniel Wildenstein: pp. iv, 16, 55, 58, 60, 64. Topham Picturepoint/Roger Viollet: pp. 51, 82/83.

Index